THE EVERYTHING
GUIDE TO BEING A
SALES REP

Dear Reader,

I grew up in a family of "shoe dogs," as my dad is fond of saying. Both my mom and dad sold shoes at a family-style store for most of my childhood. I remember going there after school and watching my parents talk, smile, and laugh with their customers. Even though they worked hard and were tired at the end of the day, their job seemed fun to me. I don't ever remember my parents saying they didn't want to get up to go to work.

True to my family, I was always selling something. In grammar school I sold salted peanuts for Blue Birds. In high school I sold holiday fruitcakes for the orchestra so we could go on out-of-town recital trips. As an adult I sold all manner of tickets for fundraising events.

Today, I am still in sales, but in addition to fundraising tickets I also sell my clients' products and services in terms of marketing and PR. Above and beyond all else, I know that successful selling is really about selling yourself first and your products or services second. It is about developing and maintaining relationships and reaching your goals by living your values. It can be a fun, fulfilling, and purposeful lifestyle—and it is worth pursuing.

I hope this book shows you something of what I have learned from a lifetime in sales and improves your bottom line. But most of all, I hope this book gives you a sense of enjoyment in your sales career. You're in a remarkable business.

Ruth Klein

D1445445

THE

EVERYTHING
GUIDE TO BEING A
SALES REP

Winning secrets to a successful—and
profitable—career!

Ruth Klein

Adams Media
Avon, Massachusetts

*I dedicate this book to all the entrepreneurial-spirited men and women
that make up the sales engine of our world economy. Here's to you,
your professionalism, and positive spirit!*

• • •

Publishing Director: Gary M. Krebs
Associate Managing Editor: Laura M. Daly
Associate Copy Chief: Brett Palana-Shanahan
Acquisitions Editor: Lisa Laing
Development Editor: Rachel Engelson
Associate Production Editor: Casey Ebert

Director of Manufacturing: Susan Beale
Associate Director of Production: Michelle Roy Kelly
Cover Design: Paul Beatrice, Erick DaCosta,
  Matt LeBlanc
Layout and Graphics: Colleen Cunningham,
  Sorae Lee, Jennifer Oliveira,
  Brewster Brownville

An Everything® Series Book.
Everything® and everything.com® are registered trademarks of F+W Publications, Inc.

Published by Adams Media, an F+W Publications Company
57 Littlefield Street, Avon, MA 02322 U.S.A.
www.adamsmedia.com

ISBN 10: 1-59337-657-X
ISBN 13: 978-1-59337-657-4
Printed in the United States of America.

J I H G F E D C B A

Library of Congress Cataloging-in-Publication Data

Klein, Ruth.
The everything guide to being a sales rep / Ruth Klein.
p. cm. -- (Everything Series)
ISBN-10: 1-59337-657-X
ISBN-13: 978-1-59337-657-4
1. Selling. I. Title.

HF5438.25.K585 2006
658.85--dc22

2006019734

This publication is designed to provide accurate and authoritative information with regard to the subject matter covered. It is sold with the understanding that the publisher is not engaged in rendering legal, accounting, or other professional advice. If legal advice or other expert assistance is required, the services of a competent professional person should be sought.
  —From a *Declaration of Principles* jointly adopted by a Committee of the American
  Bar Association and a Committee of Publishers and Associations

Many of the designations used by manufacturers and sellers to distinguish their products are claimed as trademarks. Where those designations appear in this book and Adams Media was aware of a trademark claim, the designations have been printed with initial capital letters.

*This book is available at quantity discounts for bulk purchases.
For information, please call 1-800-872-5627.*

Visit the entire Everything® series at *www.everything.com*

Contents

Acknowledgments

There are so many wonderful sales professionals whom I admire and who have taught me so much over the years, whether in person, via video, or through conferences.

First, thanks to my agent, June Clark, who inspired me to do this project; Dan McNeill, who made my words organized and spirited; Alan Klein, who was more excited than I was when he first learned about the book; Yossie Ziff, who brought in food during tight deadlines; Jerry Weiner, who is the consummate salesperson; and my beautiful children, Naomi Klein, David Klein, and Daniel Klein, who anxiously awaited the completion of this book.

I also want to thank all my mentors whom I know personally as well as those whom I only know through books, interviews, or conferences.

Thanks to my clients for sharing a little bit of their lives, spirit, and successes. None of this would be possible without the support of and interchanges with my clients.

This book is truly for all the sales professionals who take their craft seriously and conduct themselves with integrity and purpose.

To all of you: Thank you and may your successes continue multifold.

Top Ten Things Every Sales Rep Should Know

1. Your primary specialty is solving problems.

2. Follow consumer and lifestyle trends to help you understand your prospects, and customers' deeper needs.

3. Develop a team of people or businesses that can fill in for you in case of emergency.

4. Invest in your education, appearance, and helpful technology.

5. Use a month-at-a-glance calendar to plan your schedule.

6. Keep your desk clear to maintain a clear head.

7. Identify at what point in the selling process you hear "no" so that you can practice turning these nos to yeses.

8. Excellent customer service is the admissions ticket to the two best types of advertising: word-of-mouth and word-of-Internet.

9. Use visualization daily to practice your sales skills and reach your goals faster.

10. Planning and organization are directly tied to your profits.

Introduction

How would you like to wake up every morning ready and willing to go to work? In fact, what if your work was more like play? What if you enjoyed your workday so much that you did not view it as work at all? What if you arose every day knowing that you were going to solve people's problems and build relationships while doing so?

All of these options are available to you now—in a sales career.

A career in sales is fascinating. Perhaps it's because the sales process, buying habits, customer service, and consumer trends all feed into a passion for understanding the intricacies of human behavior. Sales involves trust and basic relationships between people, as well as a grasp of what consumers need and want, and it's endlessly absorbing. You're always learning new things.

Sales is also ancient. It began with the trading of goods among prehistoric tribes in Africa, and we'll never know where the first markets were or who first felt the call of sales. But full-time sales professionals were uncommon before the Industrial Revolution. Most merchants ran small shops and both made and sold their wares. However, with the rise of large companies and the specialization they enabled, sales became a serious profession. Indeed, the world could not be what it is today without sales professionals fueling the growth of the myriad products and services all around us.

Anyone can be a successful sales rep if he or she wants to be. The knowledge you'll gain from this book will help to make you an effective sales professional. You will learn ways to tap into your buyer's motivations, creative and effective strategies to go beyond consumer expectations, how to put all twenty-four hours a day to work for you, and basic tools of time management. You will learn several ways to understand the sales rep success formula in your personal and professional life, and why a sale never really closes.

To do well in sales, you need a desire to succeed, a genuine desire to help solve others' problems, a positive attitude, patience, a clear focus and direction to your efforts, a supportive work environment, persistence, consistent follow-up, and time management skills that validate and support who you are. If this list seems long, realize that each item on it is available to you if you simply try.

Introverts often say that they do not like sales; that they do not like to be "pushy" with clients. People often think that if they were more extroverted they would be better at sales. But both extroverts and introverts can become successful sales professionals. If you enjoy talking with other people, you have what it takes to get started. Extroverts typically find sales exciting and like chatting with several people at a time. Introverts, on the other hand, may find sales intimidating and prefer chatting with just one or two people at a time. But the fundamental factors in sales are building genuine relationships and helping to solve another person's problems, which anyone—introvert or extrovert—can do successfully.

Technology can help make the job of a sales professional easier and make the use of one's time more efficient. Embrace what technology has to offer you in your sales career. The Internet and computer technology coupled with personal honesty and genuineness make for a winning lottery ticket in sales.

There will always be others who sell what you sell, but there will never be another you. Your uniqueness is your brand. It is your responsibility to find that uniqueness and communicate your brand in a clear and honest way.

After reading this book you will wake up in the morning grateful for the opportunity to be in one of the best, most profitable, and fulfilling professions on earth.

Chapter 1

Selling Is Everywhere

It takes sales to move products and services. Period! That's why successful sales reps are worth their weight in gold. You just need to go to companies that depend on them and ask one question: What is a sales rep worth to you who increases sales every quarter with a minimum of cost? Across the board, companies get excited just imagining such a person in their company.

Observing Sales in Daily Life

In the mornings you may enjoy a soy latte at your favorite coffeehouse while reading the *Wall Street Journal.* As you gaze outside the large window you may see a sign in the bank window across the street: "Visualize income—5% interest." Next door is a large awning that reads: "Flowers here." Down the street you may see a banner at the Chinese restaurant: "Now Open." Within the coffeehouse walls a big poster reads: "Be Bold, Try a Latte." All these signs really say a single thing: "Please buy what I am selling."

Look around. Everywhere, someone is selling something. Even professionals such as accountants, attorneys, and financial experts, who may not claim to be in sales, are selling something. If you are representing a product, a service, an idea, or a vision, you are a salesperson. In other words, everyone is in sales.

Sales reps have a lot in common, and these common threads run through many different industries. That is what this book is about: uncovering the common denominators of top sales reps. Every successful undertaking has a formula within certain parameters, however tangible or intangible it may be.

In summary then, a sales rep is anyone who is representing a product, a service, an idea, or a vision and wants someone to "buy" it. This doesn't have to always mean an exchange of money. You may be trying to get someone to "buy into" your idea, show their support, take some action. For example, management sells its internal culture and ways of doing business to its employees.

Here are some of the ways you are selling. When you try to get your kids up in the morning you're trying to sell them on the idea of how important school is to their education and how much it matters for them to show up to class. Chances are good that you are sharing with the children the benefits of going to school and how education will help them reach their goals.

When you suggest an idea to your spouse and hope he or she "buys into" it, you're selling an idea. You not only share your idea but you listen to what the other person wants and how your idea will match up so that they "buy" your idea.

E ssential

Every time you open your e-mail, you see businesses and others trying to sell you something in the subject header. The subject header of an e-mail is one of the most important selling sentences in the entire sales promotion. Use your subject header to get your message across quickly and get customers interested enough to open the e-mail.

When you try to get your children to eat breakfast in the morning, you're selling them on the idea of eating well so they have more energy for their minds and bodies to forge ahead on the day's activities. If your kids play sports you may tell them that eating a good, healthy breakfast will give them more energy to excel in their sport.

When you're in a meeting at work, you're selling when you want an employee, a coworker, or the executive team to accept your idea. Selling between colleagues goes on all day long.

When you call a client to check up on the progress of the deal you're in, you're in the process of follow-up and customer service, two crucial aspects of selling. Each time you make a follow-up contact you have the opportunity to cement the deal.

Every time you write a report you are selling your ideas, credibility, and findings. You take the time to write a report in a way that is organized and has enough "punch" to sell the information represented in it.

When you use statistics to help support your point of view or product, you're selling. One of the main reasons you take the time to find and present statistics is that you know that outside, third-person credibility speaks volumes to help sell your ideas, products, and services.

Everyone Is in Sales

Once you recognize that selling goes on everywhere every day, it is easier to accept that you too are selling. If you truly believe that you are in the selling business, the negative emotional blockages that many people associate with "selling" evaporate and change into a strong, positive belief system toward selling. This paradigm shift makes a huge impact on your bottom line, your ability to achieve your goals, and your energy levels. This positive attitude is covered in more detail in Chapter 5.

You're dying to go on a trip with the guys or the girls. If you're married, you may need to sell the idea to your partner. If you're single, maybe you have to sell your friends on the idea of going on a trip and spending money at a time when they're wanting to save more money—you're selling.

If you drive along a commercial stretch of road, there probably is a lot of selling going on around you—the cleaners have a sign up promoting a special; the bank is advertising a new interest rate it is selling; the radio commercial is describing the benefits of a product;

a parking lot has information about a service emblazoned on a back door or window or awning; the coffeehouse is selling a variety of drinks and foods; the newspaper in the clear plastic stand is selling its stories with attention-grabbing headlines on the front page and teasers for inside sections.

Fact

Blogs, or Weblogs, are Internet sites that the sales rep creates and shares with his or her prospects, clients, and anyone else who wants to read them. Blogs have become very instrumental in reaching new prospects and customers because anyone can access them at any time.

When you arrive at your office, suppose you go directly to your first meeting for the day. The person leading it may be selling you on the idea of increasing sales with a new product, a new service beginning next month, or an idea that management wants your support on. As you go through your workday, people inside and outside your office are probably selling you on ideas, even though it may be as mundane as where the two or three of you will eat lunch or where to dangle a line on your next fishing trip. It's all selling!

Subliminal Selling

Subliminal selling involves using a third party to do the selling. It is a very creative and persuasive method of selling. People are always looking for creative and new ways to "show and tell" to get the message out about their product or service. Here are a few ways subliminal selling is used:

- Product endorsements by celebrities or experts (word-of-mouth selling)
- Product placement in movies

- Publicity-driven endorsements that use people in the public eye to "test" their products
- Editing of movie trailers for films to bring out the excitement, romance, or humor of the experience

Subliminal selling focuses on promoting a product or service without the customer realizing it consciously. It is a very powerful tool in getting others to purchase your product or service.

Your Office Is a Subliminal Selling Point

Holding an event at your place of business can be a great subliminal selling point. Companies benefit from events at their places of business in several ways. First, they provide clients and prospective clients a chance to establish the habit of going to your business. The prospects know where you are and how to get there. You want to make things easy and convenient for your customers in every possible way. Second, your office reflects your hobbies, family, your business philosophy, your organizing style. These are all selling points that say volumes about you. Imagine a financial consultant who works for a large financial firm hosting a cocktail party at his office building. His walls feature positive, motivational quotes framed prominently, and he finds out that a new client—who was only a prospect before attending his cocktail party—had decided to work with him because of the positive statements on his walls. This is a form of subliminal selling.

Subliminal selling can take many forms. If your services include meeting people the old-fashioned way, face-to-face, someone's compliment of you may be the subliminal message another person needs to decide to start working with you. You may enter a small sandwich and coffee shop planning just to buy coffee. If there are posters on all the walls explaining how different vitamins help your body, and portions of articles from national magazines about health are placed on the wall asymmetrically, and nutritional information is stenciled on and used as wallpaper, the walls may end up selling you a fresh juice!

Even if you don't have regular face-to-face contact with your customers, you can add a small but high-impact touch that helps sell yourself and your products: With every order you send out, include a little thank-you note.

How to Identify Profitable Selling

Of course you're in business to make a profit. Even if you're in the nonprofit world, you're still in business to make a profit. Without a profit, you wouldn't be able to help people or provide services and products to your audience. People in the nonprofit world often think, "We're a not-for-profit business." However, it is important to keep this question in mind: If you don't make a profit, how do you help the cause you're trying to serve?

In business, profit is the extra cash made after paying for the goods, operating expenses, and any other business expenses. A parent may say that the profit, or payoff, that they receive from their investment of raising their children is bringing good and loving adults into the world. The dictionary says a nonprofit organization is one not run for the *primary* purpose of making a business profit. Profit is not the ultimate goal, but it is still essential: a means toward other ends that are the organization's goals. Perhaps profit in this case is helping more people.

E ssential

Dale Carnegie said about profit, "The successful man will profit from his mistakes and try again in a different way." This speaks clearly to the point that part of business is trial and error, and this is a healthy business practice. Don't let one mistake discourage you.

Money is only one type of currency for which you exchange goods and services. Other kinds of currency include a feeling of acknowledgment, experience, increased credibility, and emotional satisfaction.

Ways to Determine Profit

How is profit calculated? The formula remains the same no matter what the currency: Profit is what remains after paying for products, services, time, knowledge, and expertise. It can be called the currency flow after expenses and time. There are several types of profit. Let's look at a few to understand the motivation behind selling.

Money

Businesses need profit in the form of currency—money—to stay alive. No matter how talented or skilled you are, you must make enough money to pay all your expenses, including paying yourself. You may have excellent and well-made products, but you have to make enough money to pay the bills, pay your own salary, and have enough to invest back into the business to succeed. Making good products alone is not enough. Communicating to your customers the reasons they should buy your products and services is an essential part of any sales rep's business arsenal.

The Reward of Helping Others

Nonprofit organizations' profit may take the "feel good" form of emotional currency that they get from aiding others. But this good feeling can't be their only form of profit. In other words, it still takes money to run the organization and meet their goals. Their main goal as a nonprofit may not be to make a monetary profit, but money makes it possible for them to do the wonderful things they do for their members and others in society.

The Satisfaction of Contributing

Selling an idea to your client or business is profitable in terms of emotional currency. All people in sales know how emotionally rewarding it is not only to see sales goals reached or exceeded (and thus knowing they are contributing to the health of the company), but to see their goods and services being used and helping people.

Quality or Brand

Some people buy because of the perceived quality of the product or service. Their main priority is to get good quality, and money does not play an important part in closing the deal. The currency of brand is very strong, especially among certain demographic groups. For example, a young person may buy only a certain brand of athletic shoe because he believes that when he's wearing these particular shoes, he'll do better in sports. A woman who loves home entertainment toys may do extensive research and realize that she wants the very best. She's willing to spend as much money as it takes to get what she feels is the best.

Knowledge, Validation, and Satisfaction

Going the extra mile and getting an advanced academic degree is profitable and yields further benefits in the form of increased credibility and higher salaries. People who do volunteer work often do it out of a personal passion for a particular association or cause because of their own experiences that have led them to want to help others. For example, people who have watched family members suffer from a particular disease may feel strongly about helping to find a cure or to provide support to other people going through the same thing. Parents who invest in their children's education and emotional stability with their time, love, and respect may consider their profit to be the feelings of peace and joy they get.

Helping Other People Sell

The best way to start a relationship with a prospect and to maintain a strong relationship with existing customers is to introduce people who you think can use each other's services. The more you help others to succeed, the more successful you will become. When you genuinely help others to become successful, they will look for ways to help you in turn. This is an ideal referral system.

This system is known as networking. For sales professionals, networking means making it a priority to meet and talk with as many people as possible. This includes people you come into contact with in person, on the phone, and through e-mail.

Fact

A smile is an instant networking tool—it helps put you and the other person at ease and be more receptive to conversation. Your ability to sell is based on the quality of the relationship that you establish with a potential customer. Most people are more forthcoming with information if they feel that the sales rep they're talking to is friendly.

Networking also involves introducing one group of people to another. The best and most comfortable way to do this is over a meal. At breakfast, most people are emotionally present to listen and may have more energy than at other times of the day. From a psychological point of view, morning is a prime time for gatherings of small groups with only a few people present. This way you don't bombard their morning with loudness and too many conversations to follow easily.

Lunch is a good time of the day to introduce several people at once. From a psychological point of view, most people have gotten in several hours of work and interacting with others by that point, and they're in a "busier" mode than during breakfast.

Dinners are similar to breakfasts in that they require a less noisy environment and should demand less energy of everyone present. People are tired and looking for an opportunity to unwind. They are usually emotionally available, if you can work within this framework. Try to choose a restaurant that serves lighter food, as you do not want your attendees to fall asleep after eating a heavy meal.

Throwing parties allows you to introduce a number of people to each other from several different industries and walks of life who may not ordinarily meet one another. It does not matter whether the party is small or large. The important point to remember at parties is to keep a sharp eye out for anyone not interacting or who looks bored. Giving parties is real work, but "profitable" as well, because you can build valuable and lasting business relationships with individuals whom you may not otherwise have had much contact with.

Affiliation programs are widely used online for networking. These allow you to point your customers to other people who might be able to offer something to them. It's an easy way to make a referral. If you have a Web site, then you have the opportunity to provide links to the Web sites of other sales professionals you admire and respect for their expertise and professionalism. You can create a "Resource" section on your Web site or brochure where you list your affiliates.

Giving oral or written testimonials of positive experiences with other sales professionals is another form of networking. No amount of paid advertising is as influential as word-of-mouth advertising such as testimonials. Successful sales professionals understand the importance of keeping clients happy *and* asking for a comment or a letter that they can use in their advertising, on their Web sites, and in their brochures.

Alert

Be careful with alcohol during networking sessions. Having a glass of wine with dinner may be appropriate, but don't encourage alcohol consumption among your guests or overindulge yourself. This is a business meeting for you, and being drunk or even a little tipsy can lose you the sale and the customer.

Engaging Your Prospect

It is important to engage your prospect. You want your prospect to ask for more information. You know you have a good "grab" when your prospect says, "Tell me more; I may be in need of your services," or "Tell me more about that. It sounds interesting." Now you're ready to move forward with building a genuine and trusting relationship with your sales prospect.

When communicating your sales pitch, there are two areas to focus on: verbal and nonverbal communication. Verbal communication is the actual words you use. Nonverbal communication is communicated more subtly, by body language. In effect, body language is *how* you say the words—including making eye contact, using hand gestures, the position of your body, the tone and pitch of your voice, and so on. (You'll read more on nonverbal communication in Chapter 14.)

 Fact

If what you say is inconsistent with how you say it, the other person will believe the nonverbal communication 80 percent of the time. If you say you want to help a prospect make a purchase but you have a negative attitude toward the person, he or she is more likely to react to your nonverbal communication and respond by not buying.

Are you speaking with enthusiasm? With genuineness? Or are you just saying the words because they're what you're supposed to be saying? All of these nonverbal communication factors can be picked up very clearly by your prospect. Don't believe it? Consider this: In most cases when you call someone on the phone whom you know well, you can detect enthusiasm, boredom, stress, or hurriedness in their "hello." So can your sales prospect.

Highlight Your Uniqueness

What differentiates you from your competitors? This is one of the most important areas to develop and then focus on in your sales career. The answer to this important question will help establish you as an expert in your area. It gives you the edge in your field or in your office. Everyone's uniqueness can be differentiated, just as fingerprints are easily identifiable although everyone's hands look similar. Finding your sales rep fingerprint will give you an advantage over your competitors.

Reinforce Your Brand

There are many ways to reinforce your brand and highlight your uniqueness. One of the most important aspects of reinforcing your brand is to establish a "look" that is instantly identifiable as yours. Use the same logo, colors, and style for all of your supporting material, such as business cards, stationery, Web site, and blog. You want to give your prospect and customer the opportunity to get to know you and become familiar with you outside the selling process—your external look and feel is your brand. When you see the Coca-Cola logo you instantly know and recognize the brand as something familiar, even if you don't drink Coke. That is branding.

Communicate How You Can Help Solve a Problem

People buy things because they feel a particular product or service will help them solve a problem. (Why people love to buy is explored in detail in Chapter 11.) It's all about WIIFM: What's In It For Me? On occasion, a buyer may make a purchase to help you out, but those occasions are very rare. Come up with a ten- to thirty-second spot that tells the prospect upfront how you can help to solve one of his or her problems.

Reflect Your Genuineness and Passion

It is important to love what you are doing and really believe in what you are selling. If you are only selling half-heartedly, no amount of guidance or positive thinking can help you be a top producer. So much of what makes a great salesperson is having a genuine passion for what you're selling. In other words, you fully believe in the benefits *and* want to be selling it.

Here are a few sample sales introductions that take ten seconds or less to convey:

- Daniel, a musician: "I play music that brings you to a place of reflection, calm, and magic. I do this for parties, for performances, and on my CDs. I also teach this magical music to children and adults."
- Lydia, a stockbroker: "I help busy people make more money in an industry that over the last ten years has averaged a return of over ten percent."

- Jim, an insurance agent: "I help you keep your hard-earned money and help you make money while you sleep."
- Moe, a real estate investor: "I help you own and afford a piece of the American Dream."

When do you use these short sales pitches? Any time you get a chance. You may need to develop a few slightly different sales pitches that you can use in different mediums. Look for places you can promote yourself and your product. Some of the areas to think about are:

- In conversation when someone asks what you do (whether it's in a business or social setting)
- In a tagline for your brand
- In magazine, newspaper, or journal articles that you write
- In credits of interviews that you give
- On your Web site
- On your blog
- In your e-zine

If you listen to the radio or watch television, you will find that they often give "sound bites" of upcoming news stories. These sound bites are developed and used to create interest among the listeners or viewers to keep them tuned in to hear the full story and get the rest of the information. This is the same thing you want to do with your short sales pitch. Your sound bite or sales pitch may need to be slightly retooled for social and business situations, but always be thinking of how you can spark interest in what you're selling.

Chapter 2

Preparing Yourself in Sales

Some people may be born to sell, but most great salespeople must still take the time to prepare specific strategies for selling their products or services. You may wish for a magic wand to wave through the air that will increase your sales and keep a steady stream of customers coming down the pipeline. Unfortunately, no magic wand does this. There are, however, effective preparation skills you can practice to build a successful business in sales.

Building Credibility and Income

The more focused and committed you are to building your business, the more you will hone the skills you need to make it work. These eight tips and tricks are just as appropriate for top producers as they are for beginners. The primary difference is that the top sales producers follow these techniques all the time, and most have created detailed systems for following up on them daily.

You Are Selling You

An ice cream company once thought its increased sales were due to hot weather, until it realized its bestselling store was in Anchorage, Alaska. Said the CEO, "We thought it was sunshine or warm weather that sold ice cream, but we found it's just the right people."

You will realize very soon that people will buy from you because of you: your personality, your humor, your honesty, your knowledge, your follow-up, and other personal qualities. Often, your clients will follow you even if you move to a new company, even in a different industry, because they know from past experience that you will take care of their needs and that they can trust you.

Think of all the people you presently do business with. Which ones would you follow to a new business? Ask yourself why you would be willing to do so. Be specific about what qualities you like about these particular people. The particular company he or she works for is not typically the reason that good business relationships develop. The company's name and reputation may have been a consideration at first, but then the professionals had to stand on their own. You may be attracted by their appearances, their personalities, or their responsiveness. Once you get to know them better, you realize that you want to continue the relationship, or else you feel your personalities don't mesh and the relationship wanes and dissipates. As insurance agents, real estate agents, or financial advisors move from company to company, you have a tendency to follow the ones you trust.

Believe in Your Product or Service

When you believe in the product or service you are selling, it shows. Selling something you dislike or believe has no value for customers would be extremely difficult. This would be a very frustrating position to find yourself in, because it would be hard to muster enthusiasm convincingly, and customers can sense this. It is impossible to be genuine when you do not believe in the quality or necessity of the product you are selling!

Do Your Homework

Learn everything you can about the products and services you're selling. Know what they can and cannot do. Do whatever research it takes to discover the extra value of your product, while being very conscious of its limitations. Go a step further and find ways that you can counter or overcome those limitations. Turn even the limitations into selling points. Find out what your competition provides and where your product fills in voids left by the competitors. Become familiar with trends in your industry, and stay on top of them. When you can speak accurately and confidently about your product and provide honest assessments of its features and benefits, your customer base will increase.

Be Professional at All Times

Selling is a business, and you must convey that to your customers in every action you take. Take the time each day to put on a professional appearance. Decide on the message you want to convey and consistently work at giving off that message with your appearance, confidence, nonverbal language, and supporting material such as business cards, voice message, Internet presence, and photos of yourself. Even when you work from your home office it is best to dress professionally, because you never know when you may need to leave in a hurry to meet a prospect or client.

Set Up a Schedule and Work It

Work regular hours daily, and devote specific times of the day to accomplishing different tasks. If you want to start your workday at 7:30 A.M., then do it consistently, every day. You may decide to spend the morning doing work that requires heavy concentration and choose to set meetings after lunch or in the late afternoon. You will find that there is a natural ebb and flow to your days. Maybe it works well for you to be in the office on Mondays, while Tuesdays and Thursdays are good days for you to schedule off-site client visits and meetings. You may find that using afternoons to check and follow-up on e-mails or to make phone calls works best for you. You will learn more about creating a schedule in Chapter 4.

E ssential

If you have a home office, dress up for work and keep a daily schedule. This way you're always available to meet with prospects or clients. In addition, sales reps who prepare themselves first thing in the mornings for work are often more productive during the day.

Watch Buying Habits (Including Your Own)

Become more conscious of your own buying habits by considering your ten most recent purchases. Ask yourself what led you to make these purchases and what the deciding factors were in choosing the items you bought. Write down the answers. Browse your competitors' brochures and check their telephone manner. Visit their stores in person and go to their Web sites. Observe the customers and sales reps. Take note of what other people are doing. This knowledge will help you to customize your selling style while you're familiarizing yourself with what's out there already.

Follow Up and Then Follow Up Some More

Just because you have a customer today does not mean that you will have her tomorrow if you slack off on following up and servicing her account. What are the ways that you can service your prospect or customer? How can you make the buying process easier for him? What would put a smile on your prospect's or customer's face? For example, could you offer to let him pay off a large-ticket item in several payment installments? Could you provide free delivery for a heavy product?

Most important, stay in contact with your prospects and customers so you can answer any concerns or questions they may have. Make it as easy as possible for your customers to get help from you. Use e-mail and phone calls. Send postcards. Invite them to events.

The most effective and productive sales strategy is to stay in communication with prospects and clients. Too often sales reps may worry that they are going to bother a client, so they contact them less often. More times than not this "stay-away" attitude will hurt you more than it will help. Take the initiative so that they don't have to.

Customer Relationship Management Software

Customer relationship management (CRM) software can be a particularly useful resource. This software provides a system for you to organize and record all information you have about customers and prospects. Because it is a computer program and not a hard copy filing system, you can easily search for information (such as the last time a customer bought from you and what he or she purchased) that, in the past, would have taken hours of digging through files to find. For this software to be as useful as it can be, you have to be sure to input any new information you receive from the customer. (For example, if your prospect moves or changes his or her phone number, be sure to update the information in your database.) There is a good chance that if you work for a large company, you have a CRM program available and you already know how useful it can be. This organized method of storing data will be a very important tool that can increase your ability to help customers.

The by-product of preparing yourself is that you are learning, experiencing, and modifying these skills while finding the right mix of techniques that will work for you.

Contacting Prospects on a Daily Basis

A pipeline is a stream of potential buyers who are close to purchasing your products or services. It may take one to two months before customers in your pipeline actually buy anything. Therefore, your goal is to have in the pipeline at least three times the number of people you expect to close sales on that month. The actual number that is typical varies by industry. Realtors may need to expect one buyer for every four potential buyers they're working with. Mortgage consultants may only need three potential customers for every one customer who buys in a particular month.

Realtors, mortgage consultants, public speakers, small business owners, advertisers, and many more sales professionals need a full pipeline every month. To acquire and maintain a full pipeline, stay in regular contact with current and potential clients, no matter how busy you are. Chapter 15 goes into more detail about ways to maintain the relationship, whether you're just starting out or you're a long-time sales professional.

Always be professional and polite. You never know when that person who asked the simplest questions or that person who seemed to be just browsing with no intention to buy may end up as your top customer.

Question

How can you know what a prospect or customer is looking for?
It is difficult to read your prospect's or customer's mind, but you can ask specific questions that will help clarify his needs and wants. Sometimes even the customer isn't sure what he wants, but if you ask the right questions, you can help lead him to the right solution for his needs.

If you're too busy or for some reason are unable to work with a potential customer, refer him to a colleague who can help him. Take the time to find other professionals who may have expertise in a field you don't or enjoy an area of the industry that you lack the patience for. Find those referral sources and establish partnerships with them. Let these professionals know that you're willing to refer customers to them when possible, and ask that they do the same for you. You may want to share with them the types of referrals you want, and as long as these do not interfere or compete with their own competencies, they will likely be happy to help you out.

Some sales professionals ignore or don't understand the Law of Abundance. This law states that there is more than enough work to go around, and the more you help someone meet their needs and wants, the more you will increase your own sales. The corollary to the Law of Abundance says that the more referrals you give to other professionals, the more referrals you will receive.

Think a minimum of two months ahead in your schedule. You will find that most businesses, including media, prepare far ahead for results. Magazines keep a pipeline of articles and ideas in the works approximately four to six months in advance of publication. Having this kind of foresight makes you more efficient. Thinking ahead also reduces stress, especially if you know in advance that you have people lined up to purchase your products.

In your daily contacts, consider all the methods you use to reach potential customers. Do your own analysis to figure out what is working and what is not. How many follow-through sales do you receive for each type of selling strategy you use? For example:

- How many cold calls do you need to make before they transfer into sales?
- How many fliers or letters do you need to send out to get a return on your investment (ROI)?
- How much money do you invest on the project?
- Are you considering all real expenses?

When creating fliers, for instance, there is more to consider than just the cost of the paper and printing. Don't forget to factor in the cost of a graphic artist (if you're using one), postage, your time, printing (or wear and tear on your own printer), ink, and any other areas that have a real cash outlay associated with them.

 Fact

The stress in your sales day is proportional to your headaches and inversely proportional to the salary you will reap. In other words, keep stress at bay by thinking two months ahead and doing the work now to line up customers for future sales. If you do, your income will in most cases increase. Your pipeline directly impacts your income.

You don't always have to see a direct monetary profit immediately from money you invest in reaching potential customers. Successful sales professionals will sometimes produce a flier even though they know that it won't pay for itself. What it *does* do, however, is get their name, information, and branding out to their existing and potential customers.

Picturing Your Customer Saying Yes

Your mindset matters. Going into a situation with a positive image can actually help you achieve a positive outcome (in this case, a sale). If your brain "sees" that you are successful and "sees" your customers saying yes to buying your products and services, then it becomes accustomed to these positive signals and helps you in your daily selling.

We all know salespeople who can sell almost anything. How do they do it? A significant part of "selling ease" and "selling confidence" lies in simply *knowing* that your customers will say yes much more often than they'll say no. By picturing your customer saying yes, not only do you foster a positive attitude, but you have conditioned your thoughts, emotions, and brain patterns to go for the victory!

Here are three powerful ways to cultivate "yes" brain patterns to help you in your selling:

1.   Visualize the whole selling process, including your customer saying yes.

2.   Send out the intention that you want the sale and that you will do anything you can for your customer in order to achieve it.

3.   When you get a no, simply say, "Next."

Every morning before you go to work and every evening before you go to bed, spend a few minutes visualizing your customer saying yes to you. Go over in your mind what you are saying, the feeling and mood you're in when you're with your client, and how the whole scene unfolds visually.

Emotional energy has a profound effect on your ability to sell. What you may not realize is that you can control this energy. Your emotions can go in a positive or a negative direction, depending on where *you* direct it. You direct your energy to work for you or against you, whether you realize it or not. Recognizing that you control the direction of your emotional energy is crucial to projecting a positive attitude. Become conscious of how you respond to events, people, and time pressures during the day. Do you look at them as hassles and sources of more stress, or do you see these things as simply part of life, teachers to help you make changes in your life and your work?

This shift in awareness in your thinking will substantially help you become more successful in your sales career.

Author Jack Canfield stated that every time he and coauthor Mark Victor Hansen received a rejection from a publisher for their first *Chicken Soup* book, they simply said, "Next." They had to go through "next" over 100 times before they found a publisher for what became a bestselling series! Think of every rejection as giving you a higher possibility of receiving a yes on the next call.

Investing in Yourself

It is important to remember that no one can take your education away from you. You may lose your money, your house, or your car, but you won't lose the education and experience you have attained so far.

Doctors, nurses, lawyers, financial advisors, and many other professionals often must take classes every year or two as continuing education to stay up-to-date on the latest developments in their fields. Continuing education courses have been around for decades, and you don't need a licensing board to tell you it's a good idea to take them. Even if no professional board requires you to take classes, you may decide to pursue continuing education every year on your own.

Alert

If you don't keep up with advances in your field, your competitors who keep up with the trends of the industry will no longer be competitors, they will own your market as well. Those who keep up their education will have a distinct advantage in their professions because knowledge is power.

Keeping up with your education in your industry is paramount to success in today's world. In every field, new information is being put forth every day, and it is virtually impossible to keep up with all of it regularly. New information is dispersed through a variety of mediums, such as blogs, the Internet, books, e-books, and books on tape, and no one has time to read or listen to it all. You probably have not yet met a businessperson who knows it all and does not need further information in his or her specialty.

Here are a couple of ways you can stay focused on continuously furthering your education, which is clearly important in determining your future success:

- Look for sources of education everywhere. There are classes you can take at your local community college or university, as well as seminars, conventions, and training sessions you can attend.
- Look for tapes, CDs, books, e-books, e-zines, newsletters, and Web sites that relate to your field.
- Read the newspaper.

It is important to read the newspaper for ideas about furthering your education and for spotting business trends around the country and in your community as well. If you're in real estate, read the real estate section of your local paper and perhaps of a national paper, too. What happens in one part of the country may well happen in your region as well.

Making a Daily Commitment

At the start of your day, do you already know what you're going to do first thing when you sit down at your desk? Each person has different energy levels throughout the day. Maybe you're a morning person who is able to get a lot done and concentrate easily at the beginning of the day. (Most people have higher energy earlier in the day.) If so, plan ahead the afternoon or evening before so you are prepared to work on a task that requires more effort or more concentration at the start of the next day.

You likely have an abundance of projects to complete, phone calls to make, e-mails to write and respond to, mail to open, follow-up on documents to handle, and so much other stuff every day. If you just allow your day to unfold unscheduled and do things as they come up, chances are you will not get much done in the course of a day. You'll be less efficient than if you scheduled particular tasks. If you decide ahead of time on the big tasks you want to accomplish and the important communications to get out for that day, then you'll find it easier to fit the smaller things in between them.

Use a month-at-a-glance calendar that allows you to see and plan appointments weeks in advance. Use a separate legal pad to keep a list of calls you need to make and e-mails you need to send. Organize your messages by topic, keeping phone messages and e-mail messages together, tasks together, and errands together for easy reference. Keeping your activities organized will help lower your stress levels.

Developing Your Team of Support

Develop a team of support, or your "dream team." A common trend among successful sales professionals is having a strong support system, with a variety of people they can count on for different functions. Can you identify a few team players to help you build your successful sales business? Let's look at what some of these functions are and see how you can develop your own dream team.

- **The brainstormer.** Brainstorm with someone who is neutral and won't get emotional but will maintain a clear head and offer objective feedback (and a reality check if you need one).
- **The supportive arm.** This is someone who can empathize with events in your life and remind you of your self-worth and how good you are in your field.
- **The industry expert.** This is the person you turn to who has a lot more experience than you in your field or a related one. It is someone who can point out new options you may not have thought of for dealing with customers, handling difficult situations, or reducing your stress levels.
- **The positive action person.** This individual gives you a new way of looking at things that actually makes sense. This person approaches most situations with a positive attitude, even when you may see only negatives.

- **The results-oriented team player.** This person offers you ideas for getting better results using the tools that you have, or suggests new tools or skills that can help you get better results.
- **The time-management guru.** This individual helps you stay focused and organized when you feel overwhelmed by all the things you need to get done. He or she is someone with excellent time-management skills, which you can learn from.

What is the best way to round up your dream team? Most of these people may be within arm's reach. You already know them. You just need to ask them for help.

Make a list of potential team players in each area. As you focus on this task, the right people will probably come to mind. When you focus on what needs to be done in your business, your subconscious often brings to the forefront answers that will help you create a solution. Let your subconscious help you to develop your dream team. Identify the type of people with different strengths and talents from yours. Stay focused on finding the best and most talented people for your dream team. Just by creating the space to do this, you will now "see" people in your everyday interactions who may be the right person to complement the group. You may find that the person good with numbers and accounting is already working for you in another capacity; or the salesperson who has great marketing campaigns may be at the grocery store when you're there buying a loaf of bread.

While you are not hiring these individuals for formal positions, you should let each person know that he or she is a person you feel you can count on for help if you ever feel overwhelmed or need a fresh perspective on your business or on your life situation as a professional sales rep. Contact each player, describe the position on the team, and explain why you chose him or her. Most people will feel honored that you think so highly of them and respect their opinions.

In summary, you need to prepare yourself in sales. Remember the eight effective techniques. Determine how many prospects to contact each day and how many prospects or customers you need in your pipeline on a monthly basis. Remember to stay in contact with your customers, mentally visualize your customers saying yes, invest in your education, and make a daily time schedule and stick to it.

Chapter 3

Setting Goals

Having well-thought-out plans and setting goals makes a big difference in your professional and personal life. Yet many sales reps do not take the time to think, plan, and write down where they want to go with their business, and in their lives in general. Work through all the questions in this chapter and work out your own answers. You will then have an excellent point of reference and action-oriented plan for moving forward with your career in sales.

Finding Your Passion

Do you feel passionately about something? Does your sales career inspire you, motivate you to do more, be more, or accomplish more? What do you enjoy doing that helps you experience the world with strong emotions? What would it take to make your life more passion-filled? What would it take in your selling career to make you feel passionate about the opportunities you have?

If you do not love what you do, you need to find a career or another company that you do love. You spend most of your waking hours working and devote your highest level of energy during the day to work. If you don't like what you do, then you simply won't do your best. Moreover, at some point you will find that you are not looking forward to getting out of bed on Monday and can't wait until it's Friday (when it's only Wednesday afternoon). This is not how to live a quality and purpose-driven life. When thinking about what it is you would really like to be doing, consider the following areas of your life in relation to your current situation.

- **Work:** What type of work or career do you want? What kind of working conditions and location would you prefer?
- **Family:** What type of family life do you want? Would you like to work from a home office? How can you make quality time to spend with your family members?
- **Money:** How much money do you want to make? What is your investment strategy for the short term and for later years?
- **Time:** How do you spend your time? Is your life balanced among work, home, personal, fitness, community, and spiritual activities?
- **Personal:** What hobbies have you been putting off? How would you like to spend your free time?
- **Relationships:** What type of relationship would you like with each of your family members? Significant others and friends? Coworkers?
- **Health and fitness:** How would you like to see yourself in the mirror? What size clothes would you like to be wearing? What goals do you have for your health?
- **Social and community responsibility:** It truly does take a village to raise a child. How can you contribute to your community to make it a better place to live? What can you do for the greater good of the planet?
- **Spirituality:** Where do you gain your inspiration? How would you like others to treat you? What would it take on your part for this to happen?

If you're not doing what you love, it becomes a burden for you to continue working, creating, and producing at your peak level of performance. There is a high likelihood of feeling burned out when you don't enjoy what you do most days. In addition, your self-confidence may decline because you are not performing at your best.

You can always get a job just to make money. But you might as well spend your quality, treasured time doing something you really love to do. You won't even feel as though you're working hard if you follow your passion and create the type of sales career that fits your personality, values, and passions.

Question

Once you find and follow what you are passionate about in your career, the money will follow. In other words, focus your career on what you really want to do and accomplish, and create goals centered around your values. This does not mean that you have to forget about creating a lucrative career that can give you and your family the standard of living you'd like to achieve. But it does mean that you look at the money-driven goals *after* you identify your values and the relationships that you want to create and build on in your sales career.

Addressing Challenges

If you love what you do but have a difficult time with colleagues or bosses, consider why you're having problems with certain people. Even if you are convinced it is the other person's fault, you need to know how to deal with all types of personalities, because you will meet other people with similar issues—maybe even your next customer. It behooves you to try to figure out ways to communicate or reframe the words and actions of difficult individuals so that you can move forward and up in your sales career and achieve your goals.

To understand and differently interpret the words or actions of someone you find challenging to work with, reframe how you perceive your day, events, and encounters. The source of anxiety, stress, or anger doesn't lie in the event or words themselves. Those things are neutral. The problem lies in attaching a negative judgment to the neutral action or event. When someone says or does something you don't agree with, your initial reaction may be to think to yourself how invalid or ridiculous it may be. These subjective feelings lead to feeling angry, irritated, or upset.

 Fact

Attorneys, accountants, and bank presidents are sales reps as well. A good sales rep matches products or services with the needs and wants of his or her prospects and customers. You can find successful sales reps of one kind or another in most successful businesses. Selling is the most common denominator among companies, whether it is a product or a service.

These feelings result from your experiences up to this point, how you perceive yourself, the words you use to describe situations, and the amount of stress you are under at any given time. This cumulative effect can wreak havoc with your ability to perceive events and behaviors without judgment.

Personal Vision Statement

A personal vision statement is different from the passion statement. In passion statements people often hear emotional words such as *love*, *inspiration*, and *integrity*. In personal vision statements, you create visual imagery. A personal vision statement sums up how you view the world and how you bridge this vision of the world to your present reality. How do you see yourself in the world?

Here are a few examples of personal vision statements:

- Freelance writer: "I see myself traveling the world and writing about my adventures in articles and books."
- Insurance agent: "I envision my practice increasing twofold within the next three years."
- Accountant: "My personal plan is to hire three more accountants and manage the business."

Identifying your passions and personal vision helps prepare you for creating specific goals. Write down your passion and personal vision statements on index cards first. Don't start writing down goals until you have carefully considered these two things. Recognize what motivates you and get in touch with your personal values to help you move forward on your goals.

Before you actually write down any goals and possible strategies to achieve them, remember that achieving goals often requires a transitional phase. You may find that you are not achieving your goals on a routine basis. You may be blocked emotionally, financially, or socially, and this interference may be undermining your success without your even realizing it. Your subconscious is so strong that you have to deliberately tell it who you are and what you want. The quickest way to do this is by identifying your passions and personal insights, writing goals and reinforcing them, and thinking and speaking of your goals as though you have already met them successfully.

One of the best ways to commence a transition is to write down the goals you seek in your business as well as goals you hope to achieve in terms of your personal life, your social life, your family life, your spiritual life, and your financial situation. Add any other goals that matter to you. Now you've identified what you want, but you must recognize that often there is a transition required before you can reach these goals, particularly if you have identified goals that help you "stretch," that is, get out of your comfort zone just a bit. For example, suppose you have been making $65,000 a year and one of your goals is to make $105,000 a year. Even though you would like to achieve this goal, you may feel a bit awkward writing down such an ambitious goal since you have not made this much money before. This ambitious goal pulls you a little out of your comfort zone and requires you to really work to figure out how to meet it successfully.

Perhaps you want to increase the number of customers in your monthly pipeline by 10 percent. It may be a stretch for you to consider how to do that, since you feel that you hardly have the time to service the customers in your existing pipeline. There are a few transitional phases you need to be aware of so that when they come up, rather than feel defeated, you will be better able to accept them, recognize that they are normal, and work through them without getting discouraged.

This process of transition often begins with apprehension. When you don't know what to expect or lack a specific and comfortable game plan, you may experience anxiety.

 Alert

A certain level of anxiety is helpful, since it prods you to more focused effort. If you did not experience some anxiety, you would lose a certain amount of excitement that comes with confronting the unknown. But too much anxiety is counterproductive.

The next level is happiness. Once you make the decision to go for it (whatever "it" is), you will become elated. There is a certain excitement that comes into play and gives you the adrenaline to get moving.

The next level is fear: As you go for it, you find that you may be hearing "no" more often than "yes." Any time you change directions, stretch, or try something new, if you don't get the desired response soon enough, you can start to feel dread or fear, and an anxious feeling of apprehension can set in. Give yourself a time frame to try or experiment with new advertising copy or a different marketing campaign before you call it quits. Stay focused and patient with an eye on your goal. And don't forget to track your results each time you try something new. There are no failures, just feedback.

The fearful phase is where many new sales reps stay for quite a long time. Those who can't get past this level of transition tend to move on to another company only to experience the same type of transitional change. Sales reps who get past this stage often move forward with excitement and success.

Moving forward comes after conquering fear. It is so much easier when you feel that you have accomplished this with your own intellect, courage, wisdom, and communication style. As you continue to move forward, the next stage becomes one of differentiation.

Differentiation is the stage in which you take your experience, your education, and the experience of others and modify them to your own way of doing things, taking advantage of your personality. In other words, once you learn the selling process, hear stories and experiences from others, and use your own selling experiences, you are prepared to differentiate, or create your own way of selling—taking the positive attributes, leaving behind the pieces that don't work for you, and including your personality.

Listen to experts in your industry. Pay attention when people in your industry give their definition of success and highlights the most important parts of the business as they see them. They have used their past experiences, knowledge, and hard lessons to find what works for them—their own unique method. Listen to what they have to say, how they discovered their unique abilities, and figure out how you can use what they're teaching you. Then add your own personality traits to the mix to achieve your own success.

Identify Your Goals

The best way to identify your goals in all aspects of your life is to write them down. There is a certain energy attached to writing down your goals. You'll probably find it is easier to accomplish a goal when you have it written down in black and white.

Just as you can't separate mind from body, you can't separate your business world from your personal world. To achieve a well-balanced life, look at your goals in all areas of life: work, family, money, personal, health and fitness, relationships, social responsibility, and spiritual.

Don't forget to look at the relationships at work, at home, and with yourself. For each area in which you're creating goals, ask yourself: Where am I now and where do I want to go? Many sales reps bring themselves down because they are not clear on what they truly want. Remember to think and plan big! You will be surprised to find out what you can achieve when your goals are written down, focused, and clear.

E ssential

Do What You Enjoy

The second question to ask is: If money weren't an issue, what would you love to be doing for your career? Here are some other questions to help you get started:

- How do you want to be spending your time at work?
- What specifically do you like about your job and what do you not like?
- Why do you think you like or dislike your job? Is it the daily work, the relationships, or the management style?

Money is the one goal area that most people review. Think big here but think incrementally as well. You may not be able to increase sales by ten times in one year, but perhaps you can do it in three years. Watching your income grow can be exciting and fun. Try asking yourself: In three years where would I like my income to be? Then work backward. So if, for example, you are making $35,000 a year and want to be making $100,000 a year in three years, figure out what you need to do to get there. How many products or services do you need to sell to increase your income by an additional $35,000 a year? Your incremental goal is by year two to be making $70,000. How many products or services do you need to sell in order to maintain this level of income? By year three, your goal is $100,000 or more— how many products or services do you need to sell now to maintain your desired income?

Other Goals

We all have the same amount of time as big achievers like Bill Gates, Warren Buffett, and Colin Powell. How would you like to be spending your time at work? At home? Be specific when you list activities. For example, instead of saying "spending time outside," say "hiking." To come up with ways you would really like to be spending your time, ask yourself:

- What activities have you put aside only to begin when you have more time or when the children are grown and out of the house?
- What activities re-energize your mind, body, and spirit?
- What type of a work relationship do you want with your vendors? Colleagues? Boss? Employees?
- What type of romantic relationship would make you happy? Do your present relationships motivate you or drain your energy?
- What can you do now that would help you maintain your health so you are able to keep doing the things you enjoy? (You probably know what to do already—it is a matter of taking action in the right direction.)

Being specific helps you define and clarify what you want. Think of goals as a road map that gives you street addresses and street names to follow. In addition, be alert to the direction you're going in; do you need to back up a bit, go forward more, or sidestep a few areas?

Planning Daily Goals

Planning and setting daily goals every day is easy if you use the SMVRT approach to goal-setting. This is a five-pronged approach to setting goals, and it is most productive when clearly articulated and written down. SMVRT stands for Specific, Measurable, Visualized, Reinforced, and Time-based.

- **Specific:** The more explicitly you state and detail each goal, the more clearly you will see how to reach your goal.
- **Measurable:** It's hard to manage or assess success if you do not have a way to clearly measure it. Establish touchstones, small steps to achieve by certain dates, that move you closer to your final goal.
- **Visualized:** See and feel the goals as though they already exist. Write goals in the present tense as if they have already happened.
- **Reinforced:** Write each goal on a 3 × 5 card or in a ring binder and read them in the morning when you get up and again at night before you go to bed.
- **Time-based:** Set specific times when you will start working toward each goal and when you plan to complete it.

Write down ten goals each in the categories of work, family, money, time, personal, relationships, health and fitness, social responsibility, and spirituality categories. It is difficult to disassociate any of these, because if one area is out of kilter, the whole system slips off balance. From the ten goals you've brainstormed in each category, choose the top three goals in each to actively work toward in the next six months. This is not carved in stone. If things change or a new goal takes priority, simply adjust.

Remember to write down your goals, and make them positive and as though they were already real for you. Just as children rise to meet expectations of good or bad, sales professionals also rise to what they think they can create, do, and produce. This is all part of what psychologists call expectancy theory, which says that people tend to produce their expectations, high or low.

Expectancy theory states that people will rise to the expectations they place on themselves. If you set your goals low, you will tend to reach that low level. If you set your goals high, you have a very good chance of reaching them. Expectancy theory starts with your perception of what you think you can and cannot do.

Fact

The beauty of goals and life in general is that they are not static. Think of goals as moving and flexible. There are times when you will gain more experience and knowledge about things, and that will require you to be flexible if you need to change, modify, or delete some of your goals.

Expectancy theory is closely related to self-confidence. Believing that you can do something makes you more likely to stick to it until you accomplish it. But if you believe you can't do something, you may try half-heartedly to accomplish it but then fall short only because your expectations were low and you had no confidence in your ability to achieve your goal.

Internal Goal Work

You can have the best-laid plans and goals, but without the internal work or mental motivation to achieve your goals, reaching your goals is that much tougher. Once you identify your goals you must then make the time to do what it takes to make these goals a reality. As a business consultant's mantra says: "Ideas are only as good as their implementation." Use the following equations to make your goals a reality.

Time management equals organization. Make room in your schedule to plan, create, file, and otherwise organize ideas and information.

Organization equals energy. The more organized you are, the more energy you have. Organization helps keep you clear-headed and focused, further inspiring you to move forward and achieve.

Energy equals productivity. It is very difficult to produce if you don't have the energy or motivation. Energy is the driving force behind your ability to produce results at work and at home.

Essential

Your career is only one important cog in the wheel of productivity. Each cog is dependent on the others to keep running smoothly and with minimal effort. The more cogs that are broken, the more power you need to keep the wheel turning, and the chances of straining the wheel are greater, potentially thwarting your efforts to reach your destination.

Productivity contributes to goals. The more you can produce, the more effectively you reach your goals. Achieving your goals will allow you to find success in all aspects of your life, helping you to find satisfaction with your income, well-being, relationships, and much more. Another benefit of achieving your goals is that, generally, once people hit their goals, they feel confident that they can redirect their energies and reach even higher goals that allow them to stretch even further than they originally thought possible.

Chapter 4

Managing Your Schedule

One of the most valuable assets you have is your time. You cannot make it up or add to it. You can be on this planet for a century and make very little impact on other's lives and your environment, or you can be in this life for twelve years and have a dramatic impact on many. How you use each of your twenty-four-hour days determines the impact you have.

Time Robbers

Being aware of the factors that take up your time without benefit can help you to avoid wasting time that could be devoted to expanding your business. Sickness is one of the biggest time drains. When you're sick you're sapped of energy and motivation. Living a healthy lifestyle can minimize your potential of getting sick.

It is important to keep up your immunity to prevent sickness. Ways to boost your immune system and fend off illness are to:

- Take supplements and vitamins.
- Eat well.
- Get enough rest.
- Keep your stress level down by regular meditation or relaxation techniques.
- Receive regular checkups with your health practitioner.
- Exercise.

Staying healthy means keeping a healthy body *and* mind. Treating depression costs society millions of dollars in medical bills and seriously sacrifices people's quality of life. Depression also affects the lives of those who live and work with depressed individuals. Recent research has shown repeatedly that for people who suffer mild to moderate depression, exercising for forty-five minutes a day is as effective as taking prescribed medication. Exercise also helps to get your feelings out, especially anger.

If you have ever felt anxious over work or family or for any other reasons, you know that it is very difficult to think clearly and focus, which again robs you of your time, energy, and productivity. Seek ways to reduce anxiety as much as possible.

Time Interrupters

There are many factors that can interrupt your productivity when you're in the flow of things or disrupt your train of thought. They may cause you to feel irritated or angry because they take valuable time away from more important things that you need to do. If you find that you are not getting as much work done as you would like, look for the specific time wasters that recur often. Look at your calendar and see where your time is going. Are you stuck in meetings most mornings and as a result you have less time to be out meeting with potential clients in person? What time do you actually begin working in the morning? Do you find that you end up around the coffeemaker chatting with other coworkers most mornings? This idle chitchat can suck up thirty minutes of time without you even realizing it!

It may be useful to keep a time journal. For a full week, keep a log that details what you are doing every thirty minutes. This will give you volumes of information on where your time is going, when you are most productive, and what interruptions are most affecting your time.

Most time interrupters can be turned around with a little planning, focus, and commitment on your part. You must first be clear on what time interrupters occur most commonly during your day. Maybe specific days of the week or times of day are more prone to interruptions. You may realize that certain people or meetings are responsible for most of your time interruptions. Once you identify the culprit, it is easier to do something about it.

Phone Calls and E-mail

One of the biggest time interrupters is the telephone. The telephone can be a wonderful tool for sales reps when you are in control of your phone. When your phone is in control of you, then it becomes a huge time interrupter. Many sales reps believe that they have to answer every call that comes in immediately or else they will lose customers. In most cases this is not true. Leave a message on your voice mail letting customers know that you will return their calls within twenty-four hours (and then do it). This takes some of the pressure off of your time and allows you to schedule blocks of time for getting other things done.

 Fact

There are very few areas in business where you need to be on call at all times. The rapid growth of technology has made it possible to communicate with lightning speed at any time of day or night. It is important to be in control of this technology rather than allowing the technology to control of you and your schedule.

If you check your phone messages frequently, there is no reason you can't plan a few hours of private time concentrating on something else. Even doctors are not available around the clock. Set up at least two blocks of time daily for returning phone calls. During these blocks of time, return as many calls as you can.

It is also a good idea to include your e-mail address in your outgoing voice mail message so that a prospect or customer can get in touch with you this way if he prefers. He may find it easier to write out his question in an e-mail immediately rather than wait an hour or two to hear back from you, at which time he may be busy with something else. Also, remember it is courteous to turn your phone off when speaking to or visiting clients in person.

What did people do before the wonderful invention of e-mail? Well, they relied more on the phone and postal service. As with most everything that technology brings, there are advantages if it is used wisely and disadvantages if people let themselves become slaves to the technology. Just as you take a few times during the day to listen to your phone messages, schedule several specific times during the day to check your e-mail—perhaps once in the morning, once in the early afternoon, and a third time about an hour before leaving the office. Do not check your e-mail first thing when you arrive at the office, or you will get off track for the day. Once you start responding to e-mails, sending out your own, and sorting through junk e-mail, you can lose track of time and waste an entire morning or more with nonpressing work.

Coworkers and Family

While it is generally necessary to make yourself accessible for discussions with your colleagues, if you find that your colleagues or staff burst into your office unannounced more frequently than you would like, then these exchanges can become disruptive interruptions. Keep your office door closed during the blocks of time you have scheduled for work that requires more concentration. Let people know that when your office door is shut you do not want to be disturbed. If you don't have your own office, you may want to wear a telephone headset to indicate to others that you are occupied. Suggest to your colleagues that the best way to get your attention is to e-mail you for a more prompt response.

Although your family likely provides you with immeasurable pleasure and joy, if you find your family lacking in respect for your time or your need to devote hours to your business, then you need to kindly but firmly communicate boundaries to them. You should communicate rules to your family before you get to the point of anger. Keep your office door closed and let others know that these are times you are not to be disturbed. If you have a home office, post office hours.

If you have young children at home, you may want to break for lunch two or three times a week and make it quality time with the children. Then it's back to work.

Exercise and Errands

You know that daily exercise has a number of health benefits, but you just don't have enough hours in the day to exercise and get your work done as well. Or maybe you make plans to exercise in the evenings, but when the evening comes you are too tired and lack the motivation to follow through, even though you had every intention of really doing it. Make the time to exercise first thing in the morning, if possible. Not only do you get your exercise in, but the effects of exercising work their magic all day long. Even if you don't have time for a full workout during the day, get in at least a couple of brief sessions. Exercise thirty minutes in the morning, take a fifteen-minute walk during lunch, and do a fifteen- to twenty-minute exercise routine after dinner.

You have errands to run—you need to pick up materials, drop off other materials, and make purchases for work. While your weekly errands need to get done, in order to have a successful career as a sales rep you must prioritize and multitask so that your errands do not become a waste of time, energy, and money. There are several things you can do to keep errands in check without their taking away your valuable time and energy. Cluster errands to one evening, one lunch break, or a few hours one weekend day, rather than doing errands every day or every other day. Identify the amount of time you're spending doing errands for work, home, and family. Then figure out your daily income, plus the cost of gas and the intangible but real cost of the stress caused by not having enough time to do what needs to be done. Which errands are the costliest, in terms of either time or money (or both)? Focus on the three errands that take the greatest amount of time and find ways to do each errand in half the time. Perhaps you can start making purchases online, use a dry cleaning service that offers pickup and delivery, or use a grocery service that delivers.

Clients and Customers

Do you find that certain prospects and customers take an inordinate amount of time by continually calling or e-mailing with the same questions over and over? This is where the Pareto principle, or the 80-20 rule, is important to remember.

The Pareto principle states that you can count on 20 percent of your customers taking 80 percent of your time. In other words, out of ten customers, two of them will take up to 80 percent of your time. Armed with this knowledge, you can focus your efforts on working with the top 20 percent of your most profitable customers, in hopes that the majority of time you spend working will be servicing them. The good news is that you can plan for the amount of time you will need to dedicate to these customers beforehand so that you can service these customers as efficiently as possible without wasting time.

You will learn to identify rather quickly those 20 percent of customers who will take up 80 percent of your time. Communicate clearly to your customers how best to contact you. You may prefer to have your most time-consuming customers contact you via e-mail as this is by far the most efficient way to handle these types of clients. For those clients who do not "do" e-mail, you may want to suggest that they leave a specific message or question on your voice mail so that you can have a response for them when you call back. This allows you some control over how they will contact you. Remember to always follow up with them in a timely manner.

Alert

There will be times when you have to ask the tough question: Do you want this person as your customer? At some point, you may decide that you do not want certain customers, and that's okay. You may suggest another person or company for them to work with.

Some prospects and customers need more handholding than others because of fear; they may not understand the whole process.

Focus on explaining the entire process for them from start to finish—you may even want to put it in writing for them in an easy-to-follow bulleted form so they know exactly what to expect when.

Energy Drainers

Motivation is directly linked to emotions, which play out in your attitude toward work, colleagues, family members, and everything else. When you take the time to have a positive attitude, you make way for more productivity by increasing your level of accuracy and success. Changing your attitude is often simply a matter of changing your perception of things. Take ten to twenty minutes every morning and meditate, do yoga, think of the things you appreciate, or read inspirational books. Accept the ways things are right now and work toward making them better in the future.

Energy drainers are those activities or people that pull away at your energy. Since you don't feel like doing much when you don't have energy, it is important for your productivity that you pinpoint people whom you have confrontations with: people who always criticize what you do, who speak negatively of your company, who do not respond to you in a timely manner and as a result you are working under more stress to get things done. All of these activities drain your energy, and as a result you create and produce less.

It's not just people who are energy drainers. Situations—even ones that are totally in your control—can be just as draining. For example, if your desk is a mess with files piled high and papers disheveled, the first thing you think each morning when you see it is that the mess signifies how much you have to do and that you'll never manage to find the time to do it all. This feeling will drain your energy first thing in the morning—not the start you want for a productive day.

Pay attention to your energy level when you are around certain people, places, events, and projects. Identify those people and things that energize you, and also pinpoint those that drain your energy. The best way to counter energy drains is to become aware of what refuels you and what drains you and then find ways to increase the former and decrease the latter. Gauge your energy level from 1 to 10 in each of the following areas (1 being very low energy and 10 being positive, high energy):

What is your attitude first thing in the morning? (To make an accurate judgment, ask your significant other, your children, or colleagues at work their opinions.)

1   2   3   4   5   6   7   8   9   10

How do you rate your feelings when you first enter your office in the morning?

1   2   3   4   5   6   7   8   9   10

How do you rate your feelings before leaving the office at the end of the day?

1   2   3   4   5   6   7   8   9   10

What type of energy did you have before and after talking to each of your clients today?

1   2   3   4   5   6   7   8   9   10

Identify your energy level when you first enter your home.

1   2   3   4   5   6   7   8   9   10

Identify the top three errands that you do on a regular basis, noting how each makes you feel.

1. _____

1   2   3   4   5   6   7   8   9   10

2. _____

1   2   3   4   5   6   7   8   9   10

3. _____

1   2   3   4   5   6   7   8   9   10

Identify the specific situations at home that refuel your energy and those situations that take it away.

Energy Refuelers

_____

_____

_____

_____

_____

Energy Drainers

_____

_____

_____

_____

_____

How do you feel when your telephone rings?

1   2   3   4   5   6   7   8   9   10

Look at your ratings and try to see patterns. Do you feel more negative in the evening? Are certain errands stressful? Try to find the underlying reason for negative feelings and focus on making them more positive.

Get Organized

Letting your desk pile up with unfiled papers, stacks of resource material, unopened mail, and an array of other items will surely take the wind out of your sails in terms of motivation first thing when you arrive in the morning. It is disheartening to see all that clutter. And you don't want to have to start the day by sorting through all that paper looking for the files you need. Talk about a waste of energy!

Essential

A negative attitude can hinder your productivity. It takes much longer to get started on a project or marketing piece if you're not in the mood to do it. Instead of passing judgment on tasks, recognize that completing tasks like going through paperwork or filing (even though you may not look forward to them) is just another part of becoming successful.

To stay on top of things, create an organization system. If you find that there are pieces of mail, papers, or forms that are lying around because they don't "belong" any place, then create one. Add another category to your permanent organizational file system for these stray pieces. Identify what categories are missing in your organizational plan; then it is easy to correct this by starting a new file with the name of the proper category. If this seems like too much for you to handle, bite the bullet and hire a professional organizer to help you set up a system. In the long run that is worth its weight in gold.

Take twenty minutes after lunch every day to file papers and put things in their place. This is a no-brainer task that puts little demand on your mental facilities—perfect for tackling while your body is busy using its energy to digest your food. On those days that you do not have ten to twenty minutes to organize your desk or office, put your papers in neat stacks with a sticky note on top of each bunch to categorize information for easy retrieval and filing later.

Take one catch-up day per month to focus on fine-tuning your organization system. Make sure everything is filed in its proper place. Move completed files into your archives. Sort through paperwork to determine what needs to be kept and what can be recycled. File anything that isn't filed yet. You may think that you can't afford to take a day just to sort and file. But it takes more time than a day to find "lost" material or to start from scratch on a project because you don't remember where you placed previous work.

Additionally, always keep your work space clear and neat, even if the rest of your office isn't.

The Rule of Two

How often do you work so diligently and busily all day long but at the end of the day still feel as though you really haven't done anything worthwhile? To prevent this from happening, use the Rule of Two to help you out.

The Rule of Two states that you should identify two items on your to-do list—two e-mails to write, two phone calls you need to make, and two errands that you can do so that if you get nothing else completed during the day you will feel as though you accomplished something. When you complete the first two items, then identify two more items. The Rule of Two keeps you focused on only two things at a time, even when your e-mail inbox may be full, there's a pile of notes you need to go over, and there's a list of phone calls to answer that's a mile long. When you are feeling overwhelmed and you don't know where to start, start with the Rule of Two. Focus on two projects, no matter how large or small, until you complete them. Then move on to the next two items.

The Rule of Two is a great way to focus on the real top priorities when you're feeling overwhelmed and feeling like everything today is a top priority. It is important to realize that you may not get everything done that you plan to do in one day. But that doesn't mean you can't still accomplish the top two items each day, which means making headway.

When and How to Prioritize

Prioritization is as important for your schedule as organization. When is the best time to prioritize? The answer may be different depending on who's asking. What time of day you sit down and prioritize the things you need to do will depend on your sleep cycle. Some people do their best work at night, and others find they get more done early in the morning. Plan and prioritize your day depending on when you have the most energy, and stay flexible to changing priorities during the day. If you're a morning person and this is when you have the most energy during the day, then you may want to plan your schedule the previous afternoon so you're ready to focus on getting through your to-do list as soon as you start the next day. If you are high energy in the afternoon and evening, you will want to plan your day early that morning when you arrive at work.

Checking E-mail

The worst time to check e-mail is when you arrive at your office, because the e-mails will distract you from your main focus first thing in the morning and, more times than not, will have you putting out someone else's fires. E-mail maintenance can also keep you away from starting your projects and making phone calls first thing in the morning so that you feel motivated to keep working. It is not a fun feeling to lose steam and feel anxious and overwhelmed with everything you have to do just one to two hours after starting your day. You have now given away a great deal of your control over your schedule, the power to make the time needed to complete projects, and the motivation and push you need in meeting with customers in a positive emotional frame of mind.

So when should you read e-mails? The best time to check your e-mail is one to two hours after arriving at the office. Start weaning yourself now from checking e-mail first thing. There is one caveat, however. If you get your energy up and running in the late morning or evening, then mornings may be the perfect time to check your e-mail. It will help you "wake up" and start the day with less demanding work than your other projects.

Timing Return Calls

The telephone is a wonderful invention, but you must create boundaries to your phone use in order for it to ultimately help you expand your sales business and not be a drag on your time. Generally speaking, there are two times during the day that are best for making or returning calls—approximately between 11 A.M. and noon, and between 4 and 5 P.M. The first period is just before lunch, and the second is just before your prospect, customer, or vendor leaves work for the day. During these times you've got a better chance of actually reaching the person you're trying to contact (and not his or her voice mail) than at other times of the day. However, that is just a general guideline, and you must figure out what the best times are for reaching your targeted group.

 Fact

With it becoming more and more common to have customers all over the world, it's more important than ever before to pay attention to differences in time zones when scheduling overseas calls, or even distant calls within the United States.

Scheduling your calls for these parts of the day will reduce the chance that you will miss the person you are trying to contact. Playing phone tag wastes your time (and the time of the person you are contacting) and can be irritating for both parties. It may be a good idea to give out your e-mail address when you leave a voice message to prevent telephone tag. Answering e-mails is often much faster and more efficient than returning phone messages back and forth, since both individuals can check their e-mail and return e-mail messages at any time of day or night, which increases the chance that your contact will respond by the next business day. Leaving your e-mail address when you leave a voicemail message encourages people to e-mail you with their questions or comments.

One of the biggest reasons many people don't return phone calls as quickly as e-mails is that they often do not have the phone numbers handy. When you return e-mail messages you have the prospect or customer's e-mail right in front of you and simply have to hit the reply button.

When to Delegate

Delegation is a wonderful concept, and it's especially beneficial once you get the hang of it. For many sales professionals, this is a very hard skill to master. Although it makes sense to portion out tasks to many individuals so that they will be completed more efficiently, actually implementing delegation can be difficult. The perfectionist might think, "I can do it better." Although this may be true, if you have many projects and many deadlines to finish within a short amount of time, it doesn't matter that you can do it better, because there just isn't the time to do it all.

The secretive player may say, "I want the credit for it." If you're a secretive player, you don't like others to know what you're working on, how you are doing things, or the systems that you're using. Chances are that you have had bad experiences in the past that made you feel that it is better to guard your methods of success carefully than to share them. However, not delegating some parts of your overload will only cause you more anxiety and a higher chance of making errors.

The workaholic might say, "I have the time to do it." You may be able to make time to do it, but what part of your life is not in balance? You only have twenty-four hours each day, and when you spend nine to fourteen hours working, add only seven hours for sleep (and most adults need eight hours nightly), that only leaves three to eight hours for meals, spending time with your family and friends, relaxing, and everything else in your life. You may want to ask yourself what part of your life needs more attention and then develop strategies to balance your life so that work is not taking up too much of your time.

The overwhelmed sales rep may say, "I don't have the time to show anyone else how to do it." If you find yourself working in this mode most of the time, then you may want to look at organizing systems that will help keep the different layers of things that can cause overload in neat "files." It is easy to become overwhelmed with the different array of newsletters, news bites, changing company policies, interoffice memos, new product launches, and the like. Once you have established a "home" for everything that comes your way and you've made decisions about which items need to be saved, then organizing using a filing system will help immensely as you manage these items. When you're ready to work on a particular project or pull up information, you'll know where to look for it.

The procrastinator might say, "I'll get around to it eventually." Procrastinators don't necessarily put things off because they are lazy or not accountable. People put things off for three primary reasons:

1. They feel overwhelmed and don't know where to start first; it is a feeling of being paralyzed into inaction.

2. They may not know how to do something, and the fear of doing it wrong stops them from attempting the project.

3. They may be waiting for more resources or information before starting.

If you find that you are procrastinating often, *just start*. Give yourself ten, twenty, or thirty minutes to get started and just do *something* related to the task. Once you start a project and spend time focusing on it, the mystery of the unknown becomes less intimidating, and often you may end up saying to yourself, "That wasn't as bad as I thought it was going to be."

Chapter 5

The Positive Mind

The mind is far more powerful than most people realize. Your mindset can help you realize your potential or it can limit how you view events, how you feel, what you try, and what you accomplish. Napoleon Hill writes in his 1937 book *Think and Grow Rich*, "You can be anything you want to be, if only you believe with sufficient conviction and act in accordance with your faith; for whatever the mind can conceive and believe, the mind can achieve." This is the essence of confidently working toward a successful career in sales.

Taking Control of Your Intentions

You are what you think you are. The Law of Expectancy works to help or deflate your thinking and productivity. Create positive "I" statements that reflect a confident, successful, knowledgeable, and productive you. Write them out and look at these positive "I" statements several times a day, particularly if you have had an extra draining client or two. An "I" statement may read, for example, "I have a great deal of product knowledge, I listen well to prospects and customers, and I am a successful sales rep." The goal is to equip the mind to become your biggest source of support as it leads you through the maze of your career and home life.

No matter where in the world you go, a genuine hug signifies warmth, friendliness, and positive energy. Regardless of language, skin color, culture, or profession, people across the globe recognize many of the same things as positive or negative energy forces.

Because body language and attitude are easy to read—across cultures, even—you need to do whatever it takes to stay in a positive frame of mind when you're with your prospects and clients.

If you mostly see the world as frustrating, limiting, mean, and hard, then chances are very good that you think of your life the same way and this is how you come across to your prospects, customers, and colleagues. Your thoughts have a direct relationship to your motivation. Your motivation is directly linked to your success. If, on the other hand, you see the world as a place where money, health, and good relationships abound, odds are high that you think of your own life the same way.

 Fact

Personal power is reflected in your emotions, attitude, actions, and words. You have the power personally to change your mindset. Changing your mindset requires you to change your perceptions. Every time you think or say something negative about yourself, your prospects, or your customers, stop yourself and restate it differently. Rephrase it to reflect a positive statement.

Your sales career, your relationships at and outside of work, and your emotional and physical health all depend on your attitude, which transfers into tangible actions and words. Your thoughts, emotions, attitude, actions, and words are all powerful expressions of the way you look at yourself and the world. A high level of self-respect equates to integrity in your sales career. Do you approve of yourself or not? Have you allowed your childhood history and career history to affect your self-concept, or do you say, "That's it! I'm ready to move on to a better and more abundant life and career." As Mark Twain said, "A man cannot be comfortable without his own approval."

Take negative, glass-half-empty thoughts and turn them into positive, glass-half-full thoughts: "I never get the good customers" becomes "I worked hard with this customer and I will review the selling steps to make sure I presented useful benefits and listened to what she needed." Or, the negative "I won't ever make a lot of money in this sales job" gets reframed as "I am smart, knowledgeable about the products, and a good listener. I am going to be very successful at this sales job."

Promoting Action

A writer of business books remembers how disappointed she was when her first book proposal was rejected by what she thought were eleven publishers, only to find out later that her agent hadn't shared an additional sixteen rejections with her! Every time she received a rejection letter she read a small excerpt from the book *Rotten Rejections*. She remembers one in particular. It said, "Won't sell—doesn't have enough impact." The book they were rejecting was *The Diary of Anne Frank*, which has since sold over twenty-five million copies. She shut the book, put a smile on her face, and conjured up a positive mindset.

Alert

Giving up stops you from looking for options. When you stop looking for options you are guaranteed not to find any solutions. If, on the other hand, you don't give up, you keep looking for new ways to solve problems. It becomes a self-fulfilling prophecy. If you think you can't, you won't, and if you think you can, you will persist.

A biomedical firm started with two partners and two salespeople. All the players were working from their home offices. They had an idea, they had the medical research, they had credible scientists, and they had two twentysomethings cold-calling from a list to find investors to kick-start this new company. They did not have an office or a company brochure even though they were asking for thousands and thousands of dollars from prospective investors. But they did have a strong, positive, move-forward mindset to make the business a go.

Within two years they raised nearly $1 million and had patented one of their measurement tools, and had several other patents pending.

Traits that are by-products of the positive mind:

- You're not affected by what others think of you.
- Your self-esteem is high and based on realistic perceptions of yourself.
- You keep an open mind and create options.
- You understand the Laws of Expectancy and know that what you expect affects the outcome.
- You are a positive role model for others in your industry and all those who know you.
- You attract the type of prospect and customer you like working with.

A positive mind drives persistence. You attract people and clients to you and you're able to accept constructive criticism more freely. You're filled with a generous spirit and your attitude is filled with gratitude. You expect the best in yourself and in others, refusing to settle for mediocrity.

Maintaining a Positive Mind

There are specific things you can do to develop and maintain a positive mindset. You may want to tackle one method of developing a positive mind each week, then add another tool the second week while keeping up with the previous one.

Become aware of the words and statements you say to yourself. Focus on the words that you say to yourself when things go well and when things don't go so well. Do you find that you beat yourself up? Change directions and be kind to yourself by speaking to yourself with respect and positive affirmations, whether you believe it or not at first. Eventually, your mind will begin to believe the positive statements.

Become aware of the words and statements you use with clients. Meditate or plan time to be still every day. Allowing your mind and body a time to regroup helps you to lower your stress and become more creative, because the more relaxed you are, the more creative you become. Physiologically the mind cannot think well when under stress because the "flee or fight" response takes over automatically. All the energy that would otherwise be used in creative thought is used physically to run or fight the stressor. This is why when you're under a great deal of stress you can't think of anything good to say, and then after you cool down you wonder why you couldn't come up with some great zingers.

Take personal time for yourself and don't feel guilty about it. Think of personal time as your ally and brainstorming buddy. You know your thinking is clearer when you take time off from thinking about work.

Learn who and what drains your energy. Focus on the times your stomach may slightly ache, your neck gets tense, your back gives out, or you begin to feel a headache coming on. Keep a journal where you can log where you are, what time of day it is, and whom you're around when these symptoms of stress strike. You will be amazed at what you find.

Thomas Edison said, "I have not failed. I've just found 10,000 ways that don't work." Many inventors and entrepreneurs kept working at their invention or craft and maintained the mindset of not giving up. Just think what would have happened if Edison had given up after the first 100 failures?

Everyone has a personal threshold of stress that they can deal with. It is important that you find what level of stress creates your personal boiling point and use relaxation techniques from your de-stress tool kit to calm down. Identify your emotional stress boiling point and keep your stress below this threshold. Water boils at 212 degrees Fahrenheit—what is your threshold? You want to do whatever it takes to keep your stress below boiling so that you can be productive.

Affirm you and your potential daily. There is something positive and powerful about hearing affirming and validating statements from others. Can you imagine how much motivation and confidence would be created daily if these powerful statements came from you?

Reflecting Your Attitude

Just as thoughts affect our minds, emotions, and physical health, our attitudes have a large impact on our behavior and actions. This direct link between our thoughts and our mental and physical health is gaining greater press as more and more research confirms the idea that thoughts can affect our health both positively and negatively.

One of the easiest ways to recognize the power of your own thoughts is to first recognize exactly what ideas circulate in your mind during the day. Keep a journal or a legal pad next to your bed and write down your thoughts first thing in the morning. It can be as short as a couple lines or a paragraph or as long as a page or two. Write without censoring yourself. Do the same thing in the evening before you go to sleep, and keep up the process for one week. At the end of that week, take each statement and decide if it is positive or negative. A statement is negative if it's not self-nurturing; if it raises doubt about your character, potential, or appearance. Put a plus in a circle around each positive statement and a minus in a circle around each negative one. If you discover that you are having primarily negative thoughts, examine your list and convert each negative statement into a positive one. Once you get in the habit of turning negative thoughts or situations into positive ones, it will become second nature. You will think positively without even realizing it.

The Power of Actions and Words

Everyone has choices. Even as innocent bystanders to events, people have the choice to learn and move forward or take the role of victim. These decisions affect your success. Some of the most inspirational movies are true stories about men and women who endured and chose to learn and move forward with the cards dealt to them. Are you in your sales career for the long haul? If you know in advance that sales can be rocky at times, you'll be in a better position to go with the sales flow.

Your words are extremely powerful to the people around you: prospects, customers, vendors, colleagues, and friends. Jokes that poke fun at another person are never acceptable or appropriate. Human beings hear negative statements far more loudly than positive ones. Most people respond to positive statements and uplifting people. Surround yourself with positive people as much as possible. People respond well to positive statements and uplifting words far more often than not.

In sales, attractor patterns are words that use positive and affirming statements. Detractor patterns are words that use negative and domineering statements. Your spoken words are used as attractors or detractors. The attractor patterns in sales cause people to be interested in you, what you have to say, and eventually in closing the sale.

John, a sales rep for a medical device company, wakes up in the morning feeling anxious about everything he has to do during the day. He doesn't really want to be working at his present job. But it pays the bills and allows him and his family to live in a home with all the conveniences they want and enjoy a two-week vacation each year. When he logged his thoughts each morning, he had an entry that read, "Here I go again going through the motions of working at my job. I don't see the enjoyment in much of it and I hate waking up so early every morning to fight traffic to get to the different medical offices."

He went on to write, "I would change jobs, but I don't think I could find another well-paying job like this at my age. If I can just hang in there another fifteen years, I can retire."

John leaves the house in a weak energy field, gets in the car to drive through traffic, and arrives at his first destination sales call forty-five minutes later. Do you think his thoughts have affected his emotions? Do you think his emotions will affect his words? And do you think his words to himself and to his prospect or customer will affect the sales outcome?

Creating Positive Space

Everyone need to have an area or space where they can think, create, and do research. Some sales reps do these things well sitting at their desks, others think better when they're on the road. When creating your own positive space, think not only in terms of physical environments, but of less tangible areas of your life as well:

- Home
- Work
- Car
- Friendships
- Health
- Relaxation

Do you have a space in your home to which you can retreat and read, meditate, feel calm, or weather an emotional storm? Is there an area that is pretty to look at? Nurturing? Organized? Having an organized space really does help to reinforce and keep an organized mind.

Do you have an area in your workspace where you feel positive energy and can do what you need to, whether it's concentrating on certain tasks or making calls in privacy? Is your workspace organized? A disorganized or cluttered work area will impair your creativity to some degree.

 Fact

You may want to use your car as an extension of your office. It allows for greater flexibility and helps you make better use of time when you have what you need for your next sales call right there. Also be sure to keep your car clean on the inside and outside—a clean car is much more calming than a messy one.

Do you find the people that you surround yourself with after hours, during lunch, on vacation, and at other times are draining your energy through criticism, looking at life from a pessimist's view, and generally giving off low energy or otherwise draining you? Or do they value you for being you, encourage you, and uplift your spirits?

How would you rate your health? Do you have energy at the end of most days or do you simply feel drained? Do you surround yourself with healthy food options? Do you make the time to put premium fuel in your body? How do you relax? Do you listen to TV news first or last thing in the evenings to relax, or do you listen to music you enjoy, or read inspirational books?

Mental Clarity and Vision

Ideas tend to come more easily to you when you can think clearly. In addition, when you're thinking clearly, you are less likely to make errors and you feel more in control of what you're doing. But best of all, the power of mental clarity and vision drives success. Here are a few ideas to help you realize this power.

Reprogramming

When you find yourself thinking negative thoughts, stop and reframe them to make them more realistic and positive. "I'm never going to get this right." Reframe this to: "I'll continue until I feel comfortable with my approach." "I don't know why I can't make a better living." Reframe this to: "I am going to increase my paycheck 35 percent by creating new marketing strategies for different audiences."

Deep-Muscle Relaxation

Find a quiet and comfortable place to sit or lie down. Move through each large muscle group, starting with your hands, then your shoulders, neck, head, stomach, legs, and feet. First tighten these muscles for thirty seconds and then slowly release and focus on letting those muscles relax. Focus on those areas where you carry the most stress, such as the shoulders, neck, lower back, or wherever you most often experience tension.

Five- to Ten-Minute Meditation

People tend to breathe shallowly and not from the stomach, which would allow you to take a full, relaxing breath. To focus on deep breathing, find a quiet and comfortable place to sit with your back and spine straight. Breathe naturally, but make each breath come from your stomach. Inhale as your stomach goes out, and exhale as your stomach goes in. You may need to place your hand over your stomach to help you get into this rhythm. Then focus on inhaling and exhaling while letting thoughts come and go without judgment.

Focus on Blessings and Gratitude

What are three things you feel grateful for? Think about these blessings. They are sure to put a smile on your face and send a feeling of safety throughout your body. These can be as grand or as specific as you like. "I am grateful for my children." "I feel blessed that I have a job I enjoy."

Focus on Self-Respect and Self-Confidence

Focus on building your own self-respect and self-confidence. Make a list of ten accomplishments you're proud of. Make a list of ten things about you that you feel deserve respect. Refer to these lists regularly to remind yourself of why you should feel good about yourself.

When you create internal strength, others are apt to reflect it back to you—making you even stronger. When you have internal strength you are not easily influenced by negative comments that a prospect or customer may make. You can separate your confidence in your sales technique from the prospect's anger, for example, without blaming yourself.

Now is the time to realize your sales dreams, to let your positive thoughts and attitudes propel you to the success you want.

Chapter 6

Identifying Your Market

One of the first things you need to ask yourself as a new sales rep is: Who is my customer? Before you say, "Everyone," stop and think. Even the IRS does not have "everyone" as a customer, because you must meet certain financial criteria before you have to pay income tax! Whether you rent out apartment units or sell jewelry, everyone in the universe is not your best customer. The better you target prospects and customers, the better results you will receive for your efforts—in time, money, and energy.

Who Is Your Customer?

First, there are no absolutes. You can competently define and identify your customers and still find a profitable client who does not clearly fit in with your other profitable clients. No problem—just stay alert to changing lifestyles, new widespread acceptance of ideas or products that are crucial turning points (such as when cell phones became everyone's best friend, when manicures became weekly beauty necessities, and when it became commonplace for coffee to cost $3 to $4 a cup), and the new benefits that your products or services provide (lower cost, greater availability, a cleaner and sleeker look).

Knowing exactly who your client is helps you maximize the dollars in your marketing budget. Clearly identifying whom you are trying to target makes it easier to determine the best ways to reach them. Different niche groups may require different marketing campaigns, which means spending more money. You may want to limit the number of niche groups you target to two to make the most of your time and money.

Here are a few examples of making the most effective use of your money, time, and energy, all of which are invaluable commodities. You can save money by sending out the same advertising copy to everyone in your targeted group, whether it's on the Web, in a letter, or on a billboard. If you are a stockbroker, you may want to target only people with an annual income of over $150,000. If you are selling high-fashion clothing, you may want to target the twentysomething crowd. Think about who your client is and tailor all your advertising to his or her specific needs. Spend time focused on your targeted markets only. When new prospective clients come to you who do not fall into your targeted audience, you may choose to take them on as customers anyway, or you may decide to instead refer them to another professional or company that does focus on their needs and may be able to address them and serve them better.

E ssential

When your customer is "everyone" and you market to everyone, it will be expensive and time-consuming. You'll find yourself overwhelmed with ad copy to "everyone," making it difficult to uniquely brand yourself. You'll waste your most valuable resources: time and money.

The hardest thing about finding prospects and keeping customers happy is the overwhelming feeling that there is just too much to do. The more targeted markets you sell to, the more business and marketing strategies you need.

Targeting Specific Markets

First, you need to decide whom to sell to. Once you recognize that everyone is not your customer, you can find out who your best or most likely clients are and identify what similarities they share. Here are a few ways to get started finding your target markets.

Think about your product and who is most likely to use it. Look at similar companies in your industry to help you to pinpoint industry-specific needs and wants. In addition, learn what specific groups lack, where there are gaps that you can fill with your products or services. Homebuyers are likely to be open to products such as lighting, interior decorating, feng shui, nontoxic furnishings, and carpets. Women in their thirties and forties are a good target for health products, remedies for de-stressing such as home spas, and weight-loss-related items. As you think about each group of people, you can determine whether what you are selling will be beneficial to them.

Socioeconomic Levels

Studies show that people in similar income levels of the economy share similar needs, and you can save much time, money, and energy when you know these needs for different economic strata and market directly to them. The insurance industry is an example of an industry capitalizing on this trend. Insurance companies know that as an individual's net worth increases, so does his or her need for more liability coverage. The insurance industry is targeting wealthy individuals, since their ranks have grown over the last few years, offering to cover vacation homes, art collections, yachts, and other items that wealthier people are likely to own.

Wealth-management firms have also risen to the demands of high-net-worth individuals and their desire to keep the money they have now to pass on from generation to generation by creating boutique divisions focused solely on the needs of people with high net worth.

Perhaps for what you are selling, you're aiming for a different socioeconomic group. Maybe you're targeting students or first-time homeowners instead of high-net-worth individuals, which will require different tactics and strategies to reach.

Novices

Another group you can target is people new to something. There has been a dramatic increase in sales related to information concerning new endeavors, from developing an eBay sales enterprise to marketing a real estate business. When people start something new, they have to learn the ropes somewhere. You may find a customer base among beginners in the stock market, real estate investing, computers, Web site development and Internet marketing, small business development, or basic accounting.

Targeting Generations

Generation Y is the name given to people born between 1978 and 1999. The 80 million Gen Y-ers in the United States today value integrity and responsibility and are looking for moral support. They are tech-savvy and process information quickly. They identify closely with brands, making shopping a fun experience. They respond to Internet campaigns, having grown up with computers.

Generation X is the name given to individuals born between 1965 and 1977. The 51 million Gen X-ers in the United States are independent, self-reliant, and resilient, partly because many were latch-key kids left to fend for themselves after school while their parents worked. They value education and knowledge of high-tech goods and are clearly more frugal than the generations that bookend them.

 Fact

Generation X makes up 34 percent of the workforce. A trend to keep in mind when marketing to this group is that this generation is not counting on Social Security to fund their retirement, and they're likely to be saving money for the future.

Baby boomers are people born between 1946 and 1964. Baby boomers are 78 million strong, including 28 million empty-nesters. Each one spends an average of $41,000 annually on apparel, cars, recreation, education, and insurance. They enjoy entertainment and experiences they can share with their children. They tend to respond to appeals to their youthful and adventurous side. Boomers like to know how a product will save them time, boost their energy, or lower stress. They want you to provide them with style and comfort at a good price. They are redefining what it means to be forty-, fifty-, and sixty-year-olds. They do not consider themselves old but rather see themselves as still youthful.

People born before 1946 are considered seniors. There are more seniors now than ever before because of the medical advances that help people live longer and the better care people are taking of themselves. Seniors lived through the Great Depression and the rationing of World War II, and they are more careful spenders than people in other generations. Although they tend to find shopping for clothing tedious, they buy 25 percent of all toys sold.

There is also the Millennial Generation, which somewhat breaks the pattern above. These are twentysomethings who are looking for good deals because they are starting their careers, homes, and families, and face money crunches as they start their post-college lives.

The "age wave," including seniors and the incoming aging boomers, will give marketers many new opportunities, although most still target the younger consumer. Seniors are millions of dollars strong and hold a very vital buying power in today's marketplace. This population group is frequently overlooked, yet they welcome the help you can offer and are very loyal consumers.

Targeting Gender

There is no doubt that men and women have different needs and wants. It is important to be aware of changes in marketing toward gender. For example, the building industry and its affiliates focused primarily on men for years. However, recently new businesses have sprung up in this field specifically to reach women. It's now possible to find things like hammers made in smaller sizes, specifically to fit in women's hands.

Men and women tend to differ in color preferences, feelings about shopping for clothes, opinions on traveling, hobbies, preferences for how they spend their spare time, and surfing habits with TV versus the Internet.

Geography

Many businesses use geographical indicators to determine where to open up shop. Wal-Mart, for example, rarely opens new stores in large cities, instead focusing on outlying areas where the company's target audience lives. Nordstrom, on the other hand, almost always opens its new stores in large cities, as its target audience is mostly urban.

Hobbies

If you receive hobby-oriented magazines or newsletters, you likely know the power of this niche market. Salespeople count on the fact that readers of hobby magazines likely have some core interests in common, such as fishing, crafts, gardening, or knitting, even if they share very little in common beyond that. Successful salespeople acknowledge the common interests of these readers and may advertise in hobby magazines to try to capture the hobby market.

Determining Audience Demographics

Sales reps who are aware of and familiar with the shifting demographics of the American and world populations can take advantage of their understanding of these segments of society to meet their goals and exceed profit margins. Key demographic segments include:

- Age
- Sex
- Income

When examining the demographics of your market, look for people of similar age who have probably experienced similar cultural, societal, and financial influences, which can affect buying habits.

When it comes to television, men love surfing the channels during a show and often watch several shows within thirty minutes. Women, on the other hand, prefer to sit through one show at a time. Men will surf several Web sites just for the fun of it. Women are more results-oriented when they want to find something on the Internet. Most men find shopping for clothes rather irritating, while most women find it fun and relaxing.

E ssential

Women and men can differ strikingly in their preferences, even their color preferences. Men often gravitate to blues, greens, and reds whereas women tend to favor lavenders, pinks, and yellows.

Be aware of the general income level of your intended market. Do your prospects and customers own their homes or rent? The answer is important, since it can indicate how much money they are likely to have (or borrow) to purchase large items, remodel, or spend on big-ticket items.

Psychographics of Your Market

"Psychographics" refers to a group's values, attitudes, lifestyles, and other emotional and psychological attributes. Discovering the psychographics of the potential buyers for your product will allow you to better target your buyer. For many years sales professionals looked only at the demographics of a population, but ultimately they found this approach to be insufficient for achieving their sales goals.

Combining demographics and psychographics gives you a much better picture of your market and an easier path to finding similar needs and values. Years before they considered psychographics important data to look at, marketers looked at and reported on only demographic factors such as the sex of the customer, income level, or number of members within a household. However, it became very clear that these were not the only important elements for determining a market; psychographics, or lifestyle factors, could be equally important. This led to the development of generational marketing.

Personal experience can affect lifestyle. People who lived through a divorce or the death of a parent at an early age tend to have different opinions about security and abandonment than other groups. War veterans have a different perspective than stay-at-home moms. The media claims that the 2004 presidential election hinged on issues of values. It's your job as a sales rep to help to uncover the values that are important to your prospects and clients, to help you understand what your product or service can do for them and how to make it appeal to them.

Rural dwellers typically have different needs from those of inhabitants of large cities. And the needs of both may differ from those who live in medium-size cities with 500,000 or fewer people. To understand the reasons behind these differences, consider differences in factors like traffic congestion, the time required to get places (which could determine how many people listen to podcasts during a commute, for instance), the number of people available to meet, and the variety of cultural events. These are just a few of the differentiating factors.

Trading Places

Try putting yourself in the shoes of the customer you are targeting. If your target household typically includes one salaried person who works outside the home and more than two children, put yourself in their shoes to help you gain a better idea of their real needs and wants. Moreover, you will improve your ability to understand and empathize with their budget and time challenges.

It is also helpful to look at your prospects' and customers' core values. As an example, mothers value saving time, money, and energy, as well as raising children who are healthy emotionally and physically and balancing life between family and work. By putting yourself in their shoes, you will better be able to come up with solid ways to attract this lucrative group to your store or your Web site.

One of the most important and effective tools you can use to satisfy your customers' needs is to imagine yourself living their lives, trying to get a sense of what products and services they might need or want. This is especially helpful when you're genuinely looking for why people may respond in a certain way to your products and services.

Selling to a Specific Group

Have you changed jobs in the last five years? If so, how many of your customers have bought goods from your new company (assuming you're still in the same industry or a related one)? If your customers have followed you over to the new company, chances are it's not because of the company, but because of you. You gave them an experience—service, knowledge, thoughtfulness—that they remembered and valued. So it is important to realize that your customers in your business today may be your customers down the road, too—but that depends on you and the customer service you provide. Treat your current customers as an important target group, too, just as you do the potential new customers you are trying to woo.

Chapter 7

Networking for Prospects

Sales is a wonderful business to be in. Wherever you go, you have an opportunity to meet the people who may become your next prospects. When your performance is tied to your income, your efforts have an immediate effect on your paycheck. Not many fields have this kind of setup. Networking for prospects is about "working it," and wherever you go, you can generate prospects just by being friendly and talking with people. Make networking a natural part of your lifestyle and there will be prospects everywhere you go.

Getting More Appointments

Getting appointments with potential customers is a numbers game. The more people you see, talk to, call, e-mail, and mingle with, the more appointments you'll win overall. To see how the numbers work, practice with this easy exercise. For one week, count the approximate number of people you're in contact with during the day. Be as specific as possible. Notice how many people you exchange greetings with; how many sit around you at a coffeehouse, gym, or a chamber of commerce meeting; how many you see at a nonprofit organization, golf course, or tennis court. Count even the person checking and bagging your groceries. Prospects are all around you. Have an antenna up all the time looking for people you can turn into prospects. It forces you to take the lead in introducing yourself to others. Even if those around you are not your prospects, they may know someone who can be.

There are several ways to get more appointments with prospects. One of the most popular ways to acquire prospects is to do what's known as "working the room." In a social setting, act as if you are the host or hostess. Make a point of going up and introducing yourself to as many people as possible. As "host" you want to make sure people are having a good time and that no one is by him- or herself. This is a perfect time to introduce people that you've just met to other new people you've just met. Your presence becomes powerful and vibrant. It shows people that you take charge, not obnoxiously, but in a friendly, thoughtful manner. Most of your potential prospects are interested in working with the type of sales professional who can solve their problems. Not only will you meet new prospects, you will also increase your self-confidence. And in a sales career, you need as much self-confidence as you can get.

Alert

Ask your satisfied customers for an introduction to friends and associates who could use your products and services. In addition to the "ask," designate an area on your Weblog or Web site that offers your prospect or customer a way to forward your newsletter to a friend. You're giving them a subliminal suggestion to introduce you to people they know.

Send a postcard or personal note to all your current prospects, keeping them informed of market trends and new products. Remind them that you are in business and looking for their loyalty and referrals. Follow up with a phone call and ask them for leads.

Salespeople are all distinct from their competitors, just as they all have a unique fingerprint. The trick is to communicate your fingerprint clearly and consistently with both prospects and clients. To find your unique fingerprint, identify the skills, attitude, and customer service you offer that go above and beyond the expectations of your prospects and customers.

Too often sales professionals look so hard for new prospects that they overlook the very people who brought them previous success. When you offer special prices to new customers, make sure you also offer incentives for your existing ones. Never forget your valuable customers who already buy from you. Do not penalize them for buying from you earlier by not offering them a sales incentive.

Asking for an introduction is a very effective way of finding more qualified prospects from the get-go. People tend to maintain relationships with people similar to themselves. If you find that one of your customers, acquaintances, or friends knows of a person who could potentially be one of your customers, and if you'd like to meet this individual, feel free to ask for the introduction, preferably over coffee or a meal. This allows for more time to exchange ideas and build a relationship.

Find members of the media who are interested in your area of sales and point them toward new trends, interesting stories about your products or services, or responses to stories they have written in the past. Editors and producers are always looking for interesting leads to pursue. Think of yourself as a media partner, helping them to create an interesting story. There is one vital caveat, however: Don't make the story idea sound self-promoting. That is the quickest way to turn them off.

To find "grabber headlines," look at newspaper and magazine titles from your field. The media wants to capture the attention of listeners or readers, and the most effective way for them to do this is to offer interesting headlines that grab them. If you want the media to interview you, then you need to create an interesting headline. An effective headline should make you want to find out more. Plan your press release so that the media's audience will want to know more.

Another way to network and promote local knowledge of your name and business is to offer something for free. Give something away to your prospects just for calling or e-mailing you. People love free stuff. With free items like calendars, notepads, or magnets, you can include brochures with information about your business, such as "Ten Reasons to Buy a Home and Insure It Now" or "Five Ways to Increase Your Sales in Fifteen Minutes."

Question

What information can I put in brochures to let people know about my business?
Write down the questions that are asked most frequently about your product or service and turn the list into a benefits sheet. You can carry these benefit sheets with you to give to prospects along with your business card.

Local and national papers have much useful information—read articles that relate to your field or that are about people who might benefit from what you are selling. Consider writing to editors or contacting the subjects of stories. If you read about someone who is in need of your services, contact them to let them know the benefits your service or product can provide.

Create a Signature Event

Signature events help build your personal brand and provide a perfect opportunity to stay in contact with current clients and to meet prospects. They work well because people enjoy them. The events are fun and interesting, and they tell clients something more about the person hosting them. They give you an opportunity to chat with clients and prospects. You may even become known for hosting that particular event, and if you invite reporters to it, you may get publicity in your local paper. Make the event interesting, and invite your clients to bring guests (who may become new clients for you).

By creating a theme, your signature event could become the event of the year for your clients. A signature event is an excellent personal branding tool. Your prospects and clients will begin to look forward to your yearly signature events. This is an excellent opportunity for your customers to remember you in a fun way. It is important to choose an event that reflects who you are. For example, if you love to travel, you may consider hosting an event with a world travel theme, or you could choose a specific place (like the Greek isles) as your theme. Keep the same theme each year or vary it—whatever works best for you.

You could also adopt a group activity as your signature event instead of planning an entire event from scratch. Bring your guests to the movies, the theater, or a sporting event. Arrange ahead of time to have your name displayed in the program or on the scoreboard. Be sure that all your seating is together and create a party atmosphere within the event itself by providing food and beverages.

Networking Everywhere

Always be networking. When you're traveling on airplanes, trains, or another form of mass transportation, introduce yourself to the people you're seated next to and exchange business cards. The close proximity almost forces you to get to know a little about this person, and there's no reason not to. You'll meet some nice and interesting people this way. If you're traveling to the same destination, you've even got an easy topic of conversation—ask about their industry in the city you're traveling to, or make recommendations to them if they are visiting a place you know well. Many sales reps make strong business contacts and friendships by starting up conversations with seatmates.

Once you meet people and exchange cards, they become part of your community of prospects that you should keep in regular communication with. Send them letters, e-mails, or other correspondence a few times a year. Keep these contacts organized. You never know when you may have the opportunity to do business with them.

Attending seminars is another way to help you increase your chances of meeting potential contacts. Holding a seminar of your own allows you to give out information to a large number of people in a short time. Create a seminar based on the benefits of your product or service, and offer it for free. David Bach, author of the book *Smart Women Finish Rich* and others, began his career by giving free seminars to women through his employer's stock brokerage firm. In his practice he saw similar patterns of women not knowing how to keep and preserve the money they were making, so he decided to start teaching women basic skills that would almost guarantee they'd have a large nest egg when they retired. He was able to gain their trust as a stockbroker and take on many new clients who wanted to invest through him, all because of his free seminars.

The opportunity to speak in front of a group—no matter how small or large—is another great chance to meet prospects and make contact with new people. If you speak often, people will soon view you as an expert in your field.

E ssential

If you're too nervous to get up and speak in front of an audience or you don't know how to make a speech interesting, you may want to join a Toastmasters group. This is a wonderfully supportive way to learn the basics of giving speeches. You can check it out online at *www.toastmasters.com*.

Giving speeches marks you as an "expert" in your field. It's easier than you think to find places in your community where you can give speeches. Consider local business or social organizations, the chamber of commerce, and schools. The most important thing to remember is that if you give your audience useful content in an interesting way, they will remember you.

Testimonials and Word-of-Mouth Advertising

Some of the most powerful advertising messages people pick up on are not the ads they see all day long in the form of billboards, car signs, window signs, and product placements on television or in movies. Two of the most effective advertising messages come from verbal communications with word-of-mouth advertising and third-party testimonials.

Word-of-mouth is the least costly and most effective type of advertising on earth. In fact, you *can't* buy it. People are more likely to believe positive statements about a sales rep or product if the feedback is coming directly from a friend or relative than if it comes from a sales rep or an advertisement. Many people feel that a friend or relative cannot profit from a sale, so he or she is more likely to provide honest reviews of a product or service than a sales rep or marketing firm, which would be motivated by profit. This is why it is essential to take good care of all prospects and all customers, no matter how much or how little they buy, so they will remember you and your great customer service and refer you to others. Third-party testimonials from satisfied customers are also free and a very effective form of advertising.

Cold Call to Warm Call

When you're making cold calls, you need a great starting line. Develop your opening remarks and make them strong. You need to give your spiel and then listen. The most important part of a sale is listening to the prospect or customer. He or she will tell you everything you need to know. If you're not able to tell what your customer needs or wants, you simply ask more questions and listen again. Then you solve each of her concerns. If you can't, be direct and honest with her. A customer may think he knows what he wants, but as you listen, you may be able to determine that there is something else that will work even better to satisfy his needs—something he may not have even known you offered. When you're honest and you've listened, more times than not you can give prospects and customers what they want.

Go for the relationship first, not the sale—nothing is more important in sales than developing relationships. You need to go out there and just have fun. Meet people, shoot the breeze, get to know different people in various industries, go to lunch, play golf or tennis, watch sports together, visit the theater, dine, or go to the gym. Just remember to have fun while you meet and chat with people. Believe it or not, you'll be working on your sales career while doing these activities!

Build trust by telling the truth and following through with your promises. When you first call prospects, find out what their needs are before you start asking for their business. Preserve the relationship even if you lose the sale. You may not get the sale this time around, but if you preserve the relationship you have the opportunity for referrals or for a different sale in the future.

Fact

Being a sales professional is one of the most fun and lucrative careers that exists on the planet! No matter where you go you have opportunities to talk about your products or services. This is one of the primary reasons you want to believe in what you sell and be enthusiastic and knowledgeable about products or services.

It deserves repeating: Customers will buy if you sell them the benefits of your products or services. What are the three or four benefits most often mentioned by your customers (not your manager)? Share them upfront after you have asked the customer what he or she wants and needs.

Why Your Network Is Your Net Worth

Your net worth is where your networking efforts make an outstanding contribution to you many times over. The lifetime value of a customer is what that customer is worth to you in the course of your entire relationship with him. The lifetime value of your customer makes your network priceless! Everyone in your network is not only a potential customer right now, she is a potential future customer, and her friends and family are potential customers, too.

The lifetime value of each prospect or customer can potentially be worth hundreds of thousands of dollars *or more* for you. Successful sales reps will tell you that the majority, if not all, of their business comes from referrals of happy customers. These referrals are friends, family members, and colleagues. This is the sales reps' mantra: Every customer is worth thousands and sometimes millions of dollars to you even if the average sale per product is small.

The same process is at work for financial consultants, accountants, attorneys, almost everyone. Larger networks mean greater lifetime value; as your network expands, so does your potential net worth.

What to Ask When Qualifying a Prospect

Building a relationship with a prospect can be fun and rewarding, but time is one of your main commodities. Therefore, you need to do some type of screening to ensure that you're using your time wisely and not spending inordinate amounts of time with a prospect who has no intention of buying for another six to eight months down the road. You could be using that time to sell to customers who are ready to buy now. Screen your prospects so that you make the best use of your time.

Is This Person the Decision-Maker?

Find out who will make the preliminary decision and who will make the final decision about purchasing your services or product. Buying is sometimes a two-step process: Your customer may be gathering information on your product or service and reporting his findings and opinion back to the final decision-maker. You want to try to pitch your sale to the highest person in your potential customer's organization. Don't, however, ignore an individual who is not the ultimate decision-maker. Such a person often has input in the decision-maker's assessment of you and your products or services.

What Is the Timeline?

Identify when your prospect needs to buy. Timing is important in the selling process. Many people start looking for something they don't plan to buy until "later," but when they find what they want, or get excited by their research and can't wait any longer, or find a great deal that they can't pass up, they buy now. These factors all affect timing in the selling process. Just because they say they aren't buying now doesn't mean you can't sell to them right now. Even when prospects are serious about waiting another six months to make a purchase, you must be careful not to overlook them. Follow up regularly with a phone call or an e-mail, or they may just end up buying from someone else who is more persistent or who happens to come around at just the right time.

What Is the Prospect's Understanding?

Ask what your prospect's understanding is of the product or service you are offering. His answer may reveal his emotional or financial blockages to buying, and you can respond to them as they arise. The communication tool known as mirroring back works well in these situations. After you listen to your prospect explain what she wants and needs, you "mirror back" to her what you believe she said by restating in your own words what you believe she has just told you. Doing this lets her know that you are on the same track as she is and that you understand her needs (or it gives her a chance to further clarify any points that she did not convey well). This communication tool also allows you to pinpoint any blockages that make the difference between a sale and no sale, whether they are emotional or financial. Then get your prospects to mirror back to you what you're telling them about how this product or service will solve their problem as well, using a counter to the blockage you hear.

For example, if the blockage is financial, you can offer a monthly payment plan; you can compare the price to the longevity and quality of using it over many years, or you can offer a different product or service that may better fit within their budget, for example. This is another reason you need to understand the value of your products and services, so that you can provide real counters to buyer blockages.

When you encourage the prospects to mirror back to you, they end up "hearing" what their own blockage may be, and this can make it easier for them to take the next step toward purchasing. Prospects and customers will give you a lot of specific information about their buying habits and what they are looking for in your product if you listen carefully to what they are saying. Reflecting their words back to them is an excellent opportunity to keep the communication between you accurate. This accuracy translates to a sale.

Is the Prospect Ready?

Let the prospect know the next step required to move forward, the same way you would inform a customer who said yes of the next step of the purchasing process. If the prospect does not wish to proceed further, she will tell you, but it is important that you take the lead in selling by being clear about how she should proceed if she chooses to buy from you.

Alert

> Never underestimate the "browsers" in sales. You never know when someone who is looking will be ready to buy. Also, never make assumptions about your customers based on what they are wearing. Outward appearance is not always accurate.

It is the sales professional's responsibility to move forward in the selling process and it's the prospect's responsibility to say yes or no. You do not have control of your customer saying yes, but you do have control over your presentation, asking open-ended questions, listening, and mirroring back what the prospect or customer says. That's how you can lead the customer to saying yes.

Stimulate Interaction

One of the most important things you can do at this time is to actively engage your prospect. Two primary methods are mental and verbal interaction. In practice they work in tandem, but each can be considered separately.

Prospects can easily get overwhelmed with information about your product and service, so you have to break it down into easily digestible pieces. Stay focused on sharing the two or three most important facts about the product at a time. No matter what you are selling, there are a myriad of solutions that the buyer can use. But instead of bombarding him with a dozen ways your product can help him, find the two or three features that your buyer will find most important (here's where listening closely will help you) and go over the benefits with him in detail. Using this mental interaction process of presenting the product in small pieces is even more important if you're selling online only. Communicate the most important benefits carefully with both words and diagrams. If your prospect feels overwhelmed, he may feel enough stress to walk out and "think about it" awhile before he gets back to you. It is always best to help your prospect think about the product or service while you're with her, so you can answer questions or concerns on the spot. You'll have a higher buy-through and make more sales.

Be proactive with your prospects and ask questions that you know they'll need to consider down the road. Give your prospect the benefit of the doubt and be honest and straightforward. She'll appreciate it.

Chapter 8

What to Do When They Say No

Every sales professional will hear no from a prospect or customer. You are likely to hear "no" more often than you hear "yes," especially early in your career. But successful sales people know how to cut the "no factor" back to the bone. Each salesperson finds a personal approach to minimize the likelihood that a customer will say no. The most important and effective way is to keep in contact with your prospects and customers. Return calls in a timely fashion and follow up with your clients.

Minimizing the No Factor

Always keep your prospect or customer informed of what is happening, where things stand in the process, and what comes next. If nothing is happening, let him know that, too. If the customer has to call you to ask these questions, you have just opened the door for her to say no. But when you keep the prospect or customer in the loop, you are providing necessary follow-up that makes it easier for the customer to say yes to you.

One of the primary reasons that prospects and customers say no is a lack of timely follow-up. Following up with your prospect or customer is vital. Staying in contact on a regular basis is crucial not only to the relationship but also to the sale. When people are ready to buy, they will usually buy from the sales rep who has stayed on top of the process, providing most other things are equal. The salesperson who gets in touch with them instead of making them do the work to communicate makes it easy on them, and that's important.

Always give your clients a heads-up if you'll be later than you anticipated in responding to them or finishing anything you promised. Many sales professionals try to ignore this part of the relationship, thinking that if they don't mention a delay, the prospect or customer won't get upset. Actually, the opposite is true. Keep people informed to let them know you haven't forgotten about them and aren't ignoring them, and you'll reduce the reasons your prospect or customer has to say no.

Give your prospects and customers a way to reach you at any time. You don't need to be available 24/7, but have voice mail or e-mail so that they can leave a message any time of day. Invest in a dedicated business phone line—don't let your phone ring and ring without any way to catch a message from a customer. When a prospect or customer says he had a hard time contacting you, you have given him the opportunity to say no again.

Always stay in contact with your prospect and customer at some level. Chapter 7 covered different tiers of staying in communication. When a prospect or customer has not heard from you for a while, you give her another opportunity to say no.

Always be honest with your prospects and customers. If something goes wrong, let them hear it from you rather than letting them discover the problem from someone else, or worse, simply letting them get very upset that the product or service did not match their expectations. The integrity you show by being forthright and taking personal responsibility for problems that arise will remind them of your honesty and professionalism, as long as you quickly solve the problem at that point and offer an apology in the form of a note or a gift.

Expecting Resistance to Sales

There are going to be times when you'll meet resistance—no matter how much integrity you bring to the table, no matter how well you establish the relationship, and no matter how much your prospect or customer could benefit, from your perspective, by using your product or service. Sometimes consumers will say no based on factors that aren't apparent to you, or possibly even to them. It's times like these that you ask yourself if you touched all the bases for developing the sales relationship. And if you did, remind your-self that you did all you could and that it is okay that you did not get this sale, because you did start or build on the relationship.

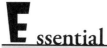

Building a long-term relationship with a customer is more important than making a one-time sale. The successful sales rep knows that repeat business is the name of the game in sales. Having a strong and honest relationship with your prospects and customers can benefit you in the form of word-of-mouth referrals and future sales.

There are times when consumers don't buy because they are wait-ing for money to come in. You may want to offer a special payment schedule to make the purchase less daunting to them and help them say yes to buying your product even if they don't have the money up front. They may have mixed emotions about buying the product or service to begin with. Help them make a good, informed decision by finding out how your product or service can assist them.

Perhaps someone is looking at what is available and compar-ing prices. Even though you feel they are "only" browsing and com-parison shopping, establish a relationship with them based on trust, knowledge, and genuine concern for their needs as a customer. They see many different products during their search and may forget some, but they will likely remember the sales professional who builds the relationship and their trust.

Talking to the Decision-Maker

It's important that you speak to the person who will be buying your products or services. This may seem obvious, but there may be more than one decision-maker—in some companies there could be doz-ens of people to sell to before you can finalize a sale. Often one per-son may appear to be the decision-maker in public when there is actually someone else behind the scenes who really makes the final decision.

Even if you don't speak to the decision-maker the first time, it is still important to make a good impression on the people lower in the chain of command, since their opinions usually influence the decision-maker's choice to purchase. But when you don't talk to the decision-maker from the beginning, you'll have to start over developing a new relationship with the person with purchasing power later in the game, when you could have been building on the synergy of all the players involved from the beginning. During your screening process you want to find out who the decision-maker is, find out what problems she faces, find out when she needs the product or service, and learn what features of your product are important to her. You need to find out the answers to each of these questions.

Take the time upfront to make sure you are speaking to the decision-maker. This will save you a great deal of time in the end. You need to be more focused and perhaps limit the time you spend with the second or third in command of the decision-making process.

Key benefits and features are important to consumers, but before they will buy, they need to feel a trusting relationship with you or the company. Above and beyond the key benefits and features is the development of the relationship itself, so continue to focus on building the relationship, meeting the customer's needs and wants as you discuss how your product or service can help him solve a problem. Focus on the benefits that best fit the needs of the client you are working with. Be sure you understand all your client's needs and all the benefits of your products so you can make smart choices about which products will serve him best.

Asking the Right Questions

It takes only a few good questions to get consumers to open up and tell you what they need and want. You'll get the most information by asking open-ended questions—questions that cannot be answered in one word. Open-ended questions require the speaker to share information. Start your open-ended questions with the words "how," "what," or "why" rather than "do," as the latter can be answered with a simple yes or no response, which does not reveal as much information. Then listen carefully to what people say as well as how they say it, and you will find out a great deal about them and what they need. If you set the proper groundwork and people feel comfortable and safe in a relationship, they will share a great deal of information. Most people love talking about themselves and what is happening in their lives. You just need to give them the opening.

It's very interesting that whether your prospect or customer says yes or no has a great deal to do with the nuances of verbal and non-verbal communication. When the two conflict, people will pick up the message you convey with gestures and intonations more than they'll believe the actual words. There is much more on this subject in Chapter 14.

Staying Positive

The successful sales rep philosophy with customers is to keep asking and stay positive. Asking can take different forms. For example, one way to ask is to do it directly. Ask for the sale in person. Another is to send a thank-you note after meeting the prospect, and still another form is to send e-mails with notices of updates, personal comments, and interesting facts about related themes.

The other factor is to stay positive. Sales professionals who stay positive and treat every customer the same, whether they buy or not, are the ones who have more business than they know what to do with. And that is a position that most sales professionals would love to be in.

Fact

Persistence outweighs intelligence many times in terms of successful careers. You can be exceedingly intelligent, but if you give up you've lost the opportunity for success. The only difference between the sales rep who succeeds and the sales rep who fails is that the former keeps working for relationships and sales.

Never stop asking for business. This can be done without being pushy. Let your prospects and customers know that you have products that will help them make money or help to make their lives easier. Continue to call and follow up.

Turning No to an Eventual Yes

Don't be discouraged even after you hear the word "no." How many times have you said no to a purchase and then turned around and bought it not long after? It happens all the time. And there are a few specific things you can do to help turn a no to a yes most of the time.

People tend to remember sales professionals who are warm, kind, and thoughtful. There is no reason not to be kind during every phase of the sale. Getting upset or angry when a person doesn't buy is a waste of energy and time. When you believe in the product or service and you have developed a relationship with new prospects or existing customers, there's no reason to be upset if they choose not to make a purchase at this time. That doesn't mean they won't buy in the future. Prospects remember the kind sales reps, the ones who took the time to listen to them and to find out what matters to them in order to solve their problems, and who genuinely wish them well even when they leave without purchasing.

And there's an important side benefit of kindness—it will also make you feel better. Dr. Paul Pearsall states, "When we tap into kindness, we draw upon our body's ability to relax and to let go. Kindness is stress-reducing behavior. Acts of kindness take our minds off our own problems. We are other-focused. When we do kind things for others, our body rewards us by releasing powerful chemicals (endorphins), which make us feel good."

Another way to turn a potential no into a yes is to create different levels of a service or product so people have more options and can choose whatever they are most comfortable with. Creating different levels of products or services allows for greater flexibility on price, added benefits, and warranties. Customers prefer to have choices when making a purchase. It is wise to offer three levels or three different price structures.

With more competition from all angles—not just brick-and-mortar shops, but the Internet and global businesses—it becomes increasingly vital to be as flexible as you can, both in your way of doing business as well as in your products and services. Ask your clients, "What more can I do to serve you?" It helps you to stay focused on what really matters: creating new ways to help your clients.

Chapter 9

Building the Relationship

The key factor in selling is building relationships. The relationship between a customer and a sales rep is the foundation of all sales, both now and in the future. Once you have constructed this foundation, you must nurture and maintain this relationship. Relationships are what sales are all about, and learning how to cultivate and continue your relationships with customers will help you to create a more stable and fruitful base in your sales career.

Finding the Common Thread

Knowing what your customer values in the buying experience is the main basis for creating a link between the two of you. It is your opportunity to find out what your prospects and existing customers value and find a way to offer it to them. Your customers make a purchase when they feel they receive some type of value that makes it worth the expense. These values may include saving time, increasing power, strengthening image, adding knowledge, increasing convenience, or solving any number of problems.

To try to get your mind around this idea, think of the last purchase you made. What was its main value?

- Was it economy—did you feel you were getting a lot for your money?
- Was it convenience—did it save time or effort?

- Was it working with a knowledgeable sales professional who helped you understand the advantages and disadvantages of the product or service?
- Was it respect and timeliness from the service provider?
- Was it the whole of the experience?

When you think like your customer you can more easily see the common threads that buyers are looking for. Everyone is looking for good value, but that can take many forms. There are several ways to provide value to your customer—the trick is to understand the way that your particular customer will find value.

New and Improved

As you walk through the aisles of your supermarket, you will find all kinds of products that have the magical word "new" on their packaging. When people see a restaurant with a banner across the front that reads, "Under New Management," many people will want to try it out, even if they've walked past the same restaurant for months without ever going in.

The fascination with "newer" (and presumably therefore "better") is very obvious in the field of electronics, particularly computers. Just when you think it isn't possible for a computer to have more storage or other bells and whistles, the most recent version seems to shout out, "Look here, I am a new and better version of the old!" Cameras, printers, and other fast-changing technology also build sales with the "new." The financial industry also runs with the "new" and "newer" packages at banks, stock brokerage firms, and other financial services. People always want to feel like they are getting a modern, useful, and high-quality product for their money. If a product is marketed as being "new," customers instinctively view it as better than other products that are presumably not as cutting edge, and therefore are willing to spend more money to obtain that product or service.

Services That Provide More

Your customers want your services, but they also want that little bit extra. The days when you could focus just on the product or service are long gone. Look for ways you can help out a customer, even if it is not directly related to the product or service you are offering. It's part of building the relationship. The more you see the whole picture in your sales careers, the more successful you will become and the higher your profits will soar because you are building strong relationships by caring about your customers' lives.

Think about what additional services you can provide that give you an added value. Do you have expertise in your field beyond the product or service you are selling? Offer your customers something extra to set you apart from the competition.

No Errors

Although it is impossible to go through your career without making a mistake, it is important to keep mistakes to a minimum. And there are some mistakes that are totally unacceptable (such as lying to your customer about the features of your product or service, being rude to a potential customer, or using unethical practices to harm your competition's business).

Accuracy is essential no matter what field you are in. You don't want to receive a letter from the IRS because your accountant blundered on your taxes, and you certainly don't want to endure a second operation because your surgeon botched the first. But even in less obvious instances, inaccuracies lower people's opinions of you. Receiving deliveries late or sending a shipment with an incorrect item gives people a bad impression of you as a sales professional. The value you can provide to your customer is the complete (or near-complete) absence of errors. Your customers have zero tolerance for errors, and having no errors will mean more sales. Check and recheck all written material, calculations, and other work before you present it to a prospect or customer. Make sure you perform in the timeframe you promised, because every moment that your customers wait beyond what they were expecting is detrimental to their faith in you as a professional. It is best to promise less and deliver more. Promise a timeframe you're sure you can handle, and then do what you can do to be early.

Create a positive encounter with your customers to create value. Your attitude and friendliness can go a long way in cultivating client loyalty. The value of purchasing at one store versus another store is often measured by people's experiences with their encounters with the employees and their attitudes. Customers may even travel further for your services over someone else's if they value your professionalism.

Effective Ways to Get Good Referrals

Why reinvent the selling wheel for every client or customer? One of the best ways to find targeted prospects that you don't even need to screen is through word-of-mouth from your existing happy customers. Ask for referrals! Let your customers know that if they are happy with your services, you'd like them to pass your name on to anyone else they know who might need these products or services. One of the best ways to get good referrals is to simply ask a pleased customer to spread the word.

 Fact

People tend to know others whom they have a lot in common with geographically and socially and who share the same interests. By getting referrals from your customers, you are getting referrals of people similar to your customers with similar buying habits.

Get testimonials and referrals for potential new clients from your customers before the deal has even closed. If your customers are already raving about you, ask then. Don't wait until a deal is closed and they have moved on with their lives. There is no better way to focus on targeted marketing than to get someone to let you use his name in contacting other people he suggests. Your prospecting now becomes a warm lead.

Asking immediately is especially important if there are several layers of other people working with you on the sale. What if the customer is happy with your role in the sale, but displeased with the next person's?

You are left in the lurch, since that displeasure may color the buyer's whole experience. It suddenly becomes too late to ask for referrals.

Testimonials are a wonderful way to capture positive customer sentiment. Post it on your Web site or use it supporting brochures or fliers. What's the best way to get a testimonial? Don't leave it up to the customer to write it himself. No matter how well-intentioned, your customers are busy and may forget or put off writing one. Instead, write the testimonial yourself using the complimentary words your customer has said to you (and be sure it's accurate!). Then give her a chance to make any changes or modifications and sign her name. *Voilà!* You have a testimonial. Ask for permission to use both the person's first and last name. It gives an added boost of credibility to have more than just a first name.

Staying in Touch

Staying in touch with your prospects and customers is vital. One excellent way is through regularly scheduled communications. This can get very cumbersome very quickly, so it's best to use a customer relationship management (CRM) software program, which can help you manage interactions with your customers. Customer management programs can also be set up to help you cross-sell products and services by helping you to identify purchasing trends in your customer base. For example, you may notice that customers paying for your cleaning service are the parents of small children. Using this information, you may market a childcare service to this same customer base.

Managing Contact

A customer management program benefits everyone in your company, not just the sales reps. It's more than just a software program; it's a system of integrating data about your customers, their needs, their buying histories, and their communications with your company. Everyone in your company, in a variety of departments, can (and should) make use of this system to help enhance the relationship with the customer.

In any business that consists of more than one person, you simply must keep track of the contact that each person in the company has with each customer to be as efficient as possible. Suppose, for example, that you help a customer today with a billing error. With a CRM system, you would make a note of this in the database. That way the next time the customer calls back, anyone who takes his call will be able to see instantly that he had called before about a billing problem and would know what action had been taken already. If you weren't tracking this information and the customer spoke with someone who had no idea what billing problem he was talking about, the customer could easily become irritated or even angry. This could lead your customer to find another company where he feels listened to. It doesn't take many of these errors to lose a hard-earned customer. CRM is a very effective way to keep track of the communication you have with your prospects and customers.

Communicating Regularly

To build a strong base of customers it is important to communicate with them in a regular and meaningful way. Forget about them, and there's a good chance they'll forget about you. One of the best marketing strategies for any sales rep is simply staying in regular communication with prospects and customers. And customer management makes your job as easy as a couple of clicks of the computer mouse. As you begin to offer new products and provide new services, or even if you simply want to invite people to a business event, you have everything you need within reach.

 **Question**

What is the solution for a firm whose customers have complained that they don't return phone calls?
Hire an excellent front desk assistant whose job is solely to return client calls to give them updates on the status of their situations. The assistant then logs this contact in the CRM software so you're able to know that the client is not being ignored.

Customer relationship management is one of the largest profit centers in your business. Once a prospect or customer knows and uses your products or services, chances are high that you can cross-sell to her—that is, sell her products that are similar or related to other purchases she has made. You have already spent the initial money and time prospecting for these new customers. Once they are in your database you want to turn them into repeat customers for life.

You can also use the CRM software to keep track of notes that aren't specifically business related. Keep track of the details of a person's life that may be minor to you but very important to them. For example, if you know the birth date of your client's spouse and children, you can call or send them a card on the date. These occasions are not big events in your life, but they're huge in your customers' lives. You know how special you feel when a sales rep remembers your name, the names of your children, or some small detail about you or your purchase after just one or two transactions. Rightly or wrongly you assume that they care because they remembered you. The importance of follow-up contact with customers should not be underestimated. CRM software allows you to keep up-to-date with any problems a prospect or customer may have, lets you know the last time you spoke with them and what topics were discussed, allows you to keep tabs on what they have purchased in the past or are looking to purchase, and so much more. The only caveat is that you must use CRM software consistently for it to be beneficial.

Making Prospects Feel Appreciated

Your prospects and clients want to feel special, to know that their purchase counts. An excellent customer relations tool is to call, e-mail, or send a postcard every few months to ask your customers how well the products or services that they purchased are working for them. This strategy keeps you in contact with your customers, helps the customer feel special, and may remind them they need to make some other purchase.

The key is to stay in contact with your clients, update them in a timely manner, and show that you care about their wants and needs. You will not believe the positive word-of-mouth and grateful testimonials you will hear—or the new clients and customers that these marketing tools will generate.

Communicating Efficiently

Let's say your goal for this year is to increase your profits by double digits. Customer relationship management can help you get there. The software lets you mine the rich information you have stored based on your key initiative and marketing goals. You easily determine which of your customers have made purchases in the last month, last three months, or last three years. You can establish a roster of "active" clients—those who have made purchases within the last twenty-four months—so you can check in with them and find out if their needs have changed. If you have kept information on your customers' children's ages, you can mine the data to find all your clients who have college-age children and contact them about what needs their kids may have as students.

Cross-selling opportunities are only a few clicks away as well. CRM lets you see quickly and easily what other products you have that could be helpful or interesting to them.

Successful reps make a point to schedule in time to keep up their relationships with clients, and customer management software is your best partner in doing this. You may want to develop a system that keeps your prospects and customers thinking of you. You might do this by developing a system in which you send Thanksgiving cards in November, offer a special discount in the spring for your active customers, and host a summer signature event.

Avoid Phone Tag

Telephone tag robs you of time—time that you could use to be selling, creating marketing strategies, planning, doing any number of things. Your prospects' and customers' e-mail addresses are only a click away.

One of the great benefits of customer management for sales reps is the ability to easily communicate with large numbers of people at once electronically. Instead of spending money to send out items like fliers, invitations, and letters, create electronic versions (or have them created by a graphic artist) that look professional and make a strong statement to your customer. Then e-mail them to the customers in your database that you're targeting. You get great, four-color pieces that would be expensive to print but that cost nothing to e-mail. Plus, e-mail is instantaneous—there are no shipping or mailing delays, so you save time *and* dollars.

With CRM, you have a variety of ways at your disposal to monitor profit. For example, which of your clients is the highest profit center for you right now? You can designate customers by categories—P1 (first-tier profit center), P2, P3, and so forth—making it easy to identify, for example, the top three tiers of customer profit centers. You have the information—you just need to mine or sort it. However, you will get the most out of it if you and everyone who works with your customers updates it regularly with accurate information.

Efficient E-mail Contact

You may be so busy with meetings with customers and colleagues that you aren't available by phone for much of the day. Or you may find that you have a hard time reaching your customers on the phone because of *their* busy schedules. Instead of leaving messages back and forth, use e-mail. People will often read an e-mail before they return a call. It all comes down to the most efficient course of action for the time that you have. You may find that corresponding by e-mail rather than phone saves time. But don't forget that e-mails can get lost or go unread. If you are waiting to hear back from someone you've e-mailed, don't let too much time pass before you follow up with a phone call. E-mail systems go down; people travel without PDAs or Internet access; there are many reasons why they may not have gotten your e-mail on time. Follow up by phone.

Exceeding the Customer's Expectations

The days when it was enough just to meet your customer's expectations are over. People have become used to having their expectations met because their expectations are not very high anymore. The advent of large superstore warehouses has trained a generation of consumers to expect little service, and many consumers have simply learned to sacrifice service for price. Many people spend lots of time driving from store to store comparing prices or buying a few items at one place and picking up a few more at another location in an effort to get the best prices. But why should they have to sacrifice service and selection just to get good deals?

The new mantra of the successful sales rep is: Exceed your customer's expectations. Competition comes from everywhere these days—not just your local shops, but national and international sources as well. To keep customers, you must do more than just meet customer's expectations. There are plenty of other sales reps who can meet their expectations, too, so merely meeting them does not make you stand out from the crowd. Your job is to find ways to *exceed* your prospects' and customers' expectations. When you do, not only will you have satisfied customers, but you will have them talking about you to their colleagues and friends, generating great word-of-mouth advertising.

On the other hand, many consumers who shop at warehouse-type stores do so because they know what they want, have done their research, and have comparison-shopped—via the Internet, by phone, or on foot. These customers are prepared to simply tell the vendor what they need and buy it with no additional input or help. Many consumers prefer this style of making purchases; it works well for them. For this reason, the best way to market to the superstore consumer is to offer them a lower price. But lower prices aren't the only thing you should offer them. The superstore that competes by also providing great service is the business that will be around for a long time with a much higher profit margin than the others.

Most consumers are aware of Nordstrom's excellent customer service and generous return policies. Even though many may perceive Nordstrom as an expensive place to buy goods, the quality of the service keeps people coming back. Costco also maintains a generous return policy and offers customers a percentage of their purchases back—both of which bring in customers.

And what about the consumers who need help in deciding what they want? They want help understanding the pros and cons of each product. The sales rep who has thorough knowledge of products and takes the time to share this information is one step closer to exceeding the customer's expectations.

 Fact

Sales reps who are knowledgeable and personable, and who can listen and communicate clearly to their prospects and customers, will never have a difficult time exceeding their goals and exceeding their customer's expectations. Create a list of ways that you can deliver over-the-top service, and implement them with every prospect and customer.

Consider creating a way for your clients to check the status of their order or view their account online. Maybe there is some additional service you can provide free of charge. What about a simple "just because," "hello," or "thank you": Call your customers every two months (or whatever length of time makes sense in your business) to ask how they're doing and if everything is working well or if they need a "tune-up." It is a perfect opportunity to "wow" them and impress them with your service. You give them your greatest asset, your time. The added benefit to you is that they may need more of your services. Anything you can do that's a little extra will mean more referrals and more repeat business. Every time a sales rep genuinely exceeds a customer's expectations, he or she makes a customer for life.

Chapter 10

Solving the Customer's Challenge

A positive buying experience is one in which the consumer gets help from a kind and knowledgeable salesperson who saves him time and money. He may not always know exactly what he's looking for, but with a little luck—and help from a great salesperson—he'll find the right product or service. Customers appreciate sales professionals who say, "No problem, I can help you." The question to ask yourself as a sales rep is: What can I do to help my prospect or customer?

Helping the Consumer

Figure out what your prospect would like and then do it. Imagine you are looking for a product or service and are having trouble finding just the right thing, or perhaps you have not clearly defined what you need or want. Then a sales rep says the lovely sentence: "No problem, I can help you." After hearing it, you know the person will take good care of you and find what you need, and you feel that the sales rep understands what you want. That is a very good feeling.

But how can the sales rep confidently say, "No problem, I can help you," and follow through on it? There must be a bridge between the knowledge of the sales rep and the needs and wants of the customer.

Understand Your Products or Services

We live in a time when knowledge is at a premium. The more information and knowledge you bring to the table, the more valuable you become to both your employer and your customer. What is driving this knowledge-based economy in the United States and other parts of the world? Certainly a primary driver is new technology and the competition and complexities that come with it. The latest advances mean that really understanding something well requires much more specific knowledge. For example, an auto mechanic today may earn a minimum of $80,000 working on cars and all the high-tech equipment that is included, as opposed to a minimum of $30,000 (in today's dollars) even fifteen years ago, before cars were equipped with so many computerized systems.

When in Doubt, Find It Out

It is your responsibility to find out how to help your customer so you can say, "No problem, I can help you." You can do this in several ways:

- Find a person who does know the answer. Call a manager, colleague, or friend who may have more information.
- Research the problem on your own. Scour the Internet. Look through your product catalog or any other place you think you may find the information.
- Provide a reference to someone who can help.

When referring a customer elsewhere, you may think you're losing a customer. The reality is you're losing a sale but not the customer, because that person realizes you've helped solve his or her problems.

Outsourcing Sensibly

Outsourcing duties and tasks to someone else in the office or at a "virtual business" is a smart choice, as it leaves you with time to perform other tasks that can't be delegated. Learn to delegate as much as possible, leaving the prospecting and face-to-face meetings with clients as your only tasks. A good way to embrace this new work model is to find creative ways to make yourself indispensable and irreplaceable. Keep up with new technology that affects your field and stay on top of the trends in fields that complement your industry. Know as much as you can about what is happening in your field and related ones. The next area to focus on is how to use that knowledge to provide a high level of service.

Keeping Records of Customer Needs

Learn about your customers. Keep records of their ages, socioeconomic levels, and even the industries that they're in. The information that you cull about your prospects and clients is monumental in terms of helping you understand who exactly makes up your customer base, helping you better screen prospects, and boosting your bottom line. Put these details about your customers in your customer management software. A simple form in your database might look like this:

Name _____

E-mail: _____

Address: _____

Age: _____

Socioeconomics: _____

Job: _____

Hobbies: _____

Needs: _____

Successful sales reps also have to look for the common messages they're getting from prospects and customers. For instance, do you find that many of them want and need the same things? Do different customers tend to ask for similar things? Is there a common thread in the requests that your customers make of you frequently? To pin down these insights, keep a journal or other record of what your prospects and customers say about your products and services—both the service they want and the service you give them. Look for ways to answer their questions before they even have a chance to ask them. And ask one additional question that is vital to the selling process: What else can I do for this prospect or customer?

Analyzing Service Comments

Take note of what prospects say about the service they receive in general. If you're hearing, "Thank you for taking the time to explain the differences in these products to me," you know that explaining the differences is important to all potential customers.

Once you analyze the notes you have written on what your prospects and customers are saying, note how many prospects you converted into customers. You may find that prospects who compliment you on your service are the prospects you end up converting into customers. Ask yourself what else you can offer your prospect. The answer may be as simple as keeping in contact with her monthly and going over your new products or services as soon as they're available. As you keep records of these questions and any others you feel are important to ask, you will see a trend in the type of prospect who is converted into a customer and the type of customer who buys multiple products or services. This insight can save you time and energy by helping you know where to focus your efforts to get more sales. Today's marketplace is different. Understanding the psychological motivation of your prospects is necessary to succeed in this new economy. It is no longer about simply having a good product or service and waiting for people to buy it.

Alert

Documenting and understanding the psychological motivations of your prospects and customers and knowing what drives them is necessary for you to make successful sales. Keep separate records for prospects and customers so you can analyze the two groups separately, and always document customer conversations.

Consulting Feedback

Finding out what motivates your customers is priceless marketing information. Consult your notes often, as this knowledge will repeatedly come in handy and help you in your sales career, no matter what you are selling. The knowledge you gain from customer feedback will help you to sell your products or services and help you to define your brand and know how it is perceived by your market. You will be able to spot patterns in who is buying from you in terms of demographics and psychographics. Stay aware of the selling process at all times. Bridge your knowledge and service and find ways to make the most of the feedback you receive from customers.

Always ask yourself the question: "What more can I do for this prospect or customer?" Can you set up easy financing? Arrange for a moving service at the close of a house sale? Call another store to have it send a product to your store? Offer other value-added services? See what more you can do.

Avoiding Excuses

You help your customers de-stress by meeting their needs and solving their problems. Chances are high that your prospects and customers are pressed for time. You can count on this being the case in most purchasing decisions. They are extremely busy, and they would rather not have to take the time to make these purchases. How can you save them time in the buying process? Make it easy and make it simple for them.

You do not need to pretend that there will never be an occasion where you need to change around your schedule or reschedule a meeting that you have planned with a customer. Things come up, and people understand this. The best thing to do when these moments occur is not to make excuses to your customer with lengthy explanations of the problems that are causing you to adjust your schedule. Instead, let your customer know as early as possible about the necessary delay or cancellation, and be sure to apologize for the inconvenience the time change may cause her. That's it. No excuses. Do not let cancellations become a habit, but if you deal with delays professionally and in a timely manner, you will not lose a customer as a result of a cancellation. Put your customer's needs and schedule first.

The Best Ways to "Just Solve It"

The prospect or customer is coming to you to solve some problem or enhance a situation for him. The bottom line is that your prospect does not want to hear excuses, which means you have an opportunity to stand above your competition by solving his problem.

E ssential

You have the opportunity to stand above your competitors with every prospect and customer whom you come in contact with. Even if your customers can get the information elsewhere, be the one they come to for information. Don't just tell them where they can get it, get it for them.

There is no replacement for honesty and professionalism. The one constant that you bring to every client and every situation is your character and integrity. When your prospects, customers, vendors, colleagues, and others know you are honest and professional, and can count on you, then you are working toward a successful sales career for the long haul.

How Promptness Fits into the Mix

Everyone knows how important an extra five minutes can be when you're rushing to complete a project, make one last call, return one more e-mail, and complete myriad other tasks. Time is a commodity that simply cannot be replaced. You would not think of stealing a candy bar, yet when you make people wait for you, you are in effect stealing time from them. Everyone knows friends and clients who are habitually ten to fifteen minutes late—and you likely think of them as being less reliable and less professional than the people you know who value promptness. Always be on time, and never make a customer wait for you.

Customers: What's in It for Me?

Customers often shop with one question in mind: What's in it for me? Customers buy for a number of reasons, including to save time, to get pleasure, to make money, to celebrate an event, to have the experience, to achieve a certain "look," and to gain credibility. All these things can be seen as genuine benefits for customers.

The disconnect in sales can arise when sales reps try to sell people the features, and not the benefits, of a product or service. It's an important distinction to keep in mind. Benefits and features are not the same.

People buy benefits, not features. A large engine in a red car is a feature. But looking sexy, hip, and rich when you're driving it are benefits that come with the purchase of that red car with a powerful engine. Brand-new kitchen countertops and high-end stainless steel appliances are features, but looking like a gourmet chef, looking wealthy or trendy, and having more space in the kitchen are all benefits of a kitchen remodel. The lower interest rate of a home equity loan is great, but it's a feature; having more money to buy a boat and vacation home while you're repairing and upgrading the bathrooms are benefits of a home equity loan with a lower interest rate. Think of the benefits your products or services offer and focus on showcasing these. Your customers buy benefits.

Communicating Clearly

Miscommunication is the number two reason sales are lost, after lack of follow-up (covered in Chapter 15). If prospects' and customers' needs and wants are not met, then they feel misunderstood on many levels. There are three invaluable communication tools that the salesperson can use as part of her professional arsenal: mirroring back, validating what has been said, and empathizing with feelings.

Miscommunication is the main culprit in poor customer-service ratings. The primary problem in many discussions in sales is that neither party stops to make sure she understands what the other person is saying. As the sales rep, you must check in several times during the communication process to make certain you really understand what your prospects and customers are saying to you.

Mirror Back

When your prospect or customer says he wants or needs your product or service, mirror back to him what you think you heard say. Rephrase it in your own words. This communication will tell you right off the bat if you are on the same wavelength. If your comments are not in sync with what your customer said, he will respond with something like "No, that is not what I mean," and then go on to clarify what he's trying to tell you.

For example, a customer may say, "I have two printers that serve as copiers and scanners. I am looking for better quality printing in my finished products. Which of these printers will do that?" The salesperson would say, "You're looking for a separate printer that will provide laser quality letters. Is that correct?"

The customer at this point can either confirm that that's what she meant, or she can rephrase what she's trying to say. And you keep mirroring back what you think she says until you are both on the same track. When you use mirroring with your customer, you prevent miscommunication right from the beginning of the relationship.

Validate What Has Been Said

Always allow your prospects or customers to state their opinions, wants, and needs without judging them or making them feel foolish for what they're expressing. A salesperson might say, "I see that you are looking for the best print quality for your printed materials." Here, too, the customer has a chance to agree or disagree. If the customer disagrees, he will let you know, and this is your second line of defense against potential miscommunication. By acknowledging your customer's statements about your product or service as valid, you are showing the customer that you value their needs.

Empathize with Feelings

Empathizing with your customers' feelings doesn't necessarily mean sharing those feelings yourself. But if you put yourself in their position, you'll have a better idea of where they are coming from and you may be able to connect better. Try to understand how they're feeling and you will better be able to know what the best way to respond is. The most important thing to remember when you're empathizing with your customer's feelings is to validate whatever feelings they express. It is not up to you to negate their feelings, no matter if you agree or disagree. Don't try to argue or convince them they shouldn't feel a certain way.

 Fact

> Prospects and customers have the right to how they feel. Even though you may not feel the same or if you can't understand why they feel a certain way, it is imperative that you acknowledge what they're saying. Mirror back to them what they say they're feeling.

It behooves the sales professional to understand these invaluable communication tools. Be part of the solution for your customers. When you do what you can to assist prospects and say, "No problem, I can help you," you're on your way to making and retaining customers. As you please more and more customers by solving their problems, you'll see a direct reflection in your paycheck. It is your responsibility to be as knowledgeable as you can about your product or service, and offer creative ways to use that knowledge to solve your customers' problems. You are human and at times you simply won't know the answer to a customer's question. That's fine—as long as you take the time to find out and get back to the customer with an answer.

Take advantage of all the information out there on the different buying habits and behaviors of your target market. Pay attention to trends both in your industry and in related ones. Remember that people buy because of the perceived benefits—not the features—of the product or service that you are selling. Listen to what they say they need and want, then create an excellent experience for them, so that they feel you understand what they need and that you care about providing it to them. And finally, use the three tools of mirroring back, validation, and empathizing with feelings to prevent miscommunication between you and your customers.

Chapter 11

Why People Love to Buy

Have you noticed that some products and services seem to fly out the door without much selling? That little eatery with the line of people waiting in the morning and during lunch may not be any better than another less-busy spot. Why are some coffeehouses filled with waiting lines to purchase $3 coffees while others aren't? How do you explain the popularity of iPods or Lance Armstrong's "Live Strong" wristbands, and hybrid cars that sell for $4,000 over the asking price? The answer lies in buyer motivation.

Buyer Motivations

People buy products and services for a variety of reasons, and their motivations may change from month to month. Buyer motivations are driven by life cycles, trends, and individual goals. There are, however, several key reasons people buy, including:

- Cost
- Quality
- Prestige
- Credibility
- Convenience
- Time savings
- Money savings
- Innovation
- Ease of use

- The opportunity to be a trendsetter
- Reliability

Money matters, and a lot of people are very price-conscious. Some are interested solely in price—getting the lowest possible price is the most important thing to them, even at the expense of other things. The market has filled the niche for this type of buyer with the large warehouse and outlet stores that have become huge successes in most industries such as groceries, clothes, and technology gadgets. Even the health industry has capitalized on this trend of marketing to those who are looking for the best price with HMOs and generic drugs.

Quality of Product or Service

Some buyers focus mostly on the quality of the product or service. Getting good quality is more important than getting a low price. These buyers will pay the extra dollars if they perceive they are buying quality—like dinner at a top restaurant—or that the purchase will last longer or serve them better than another, cheaper product.

Everyone is familiar with restaurants, clothing stores, and other establishments that carry a certain prestige. Prestige is different from quality. People will patronize a restaurant with prestige because they like its image or want to be seen there, regardless of how they like the food. They'll go to a high-quality restaurant because they love the food.

Credible Name and Convenience

Sometimes people will buy because a product comes from a credible, solid company. If a company has consistently provided quality products to customers, the customers associate the name of the company with that high standard of quality and are more likely to buy from that company repeatedly. As discussed in Chapter 2, customers will buy because of you, your honesty, capacity, and reputation for service. Credibility is priceless.

Have you ever paid more money at a convenience store just to avoid the long lines at the supermarket? That's one way that people may be willing to pay more for convenience. These buyers want what they want without having to go out of their way to get it or without having to waste time standing in line for it. If you can make it convenient for your buyer to buy from you, you increase the chances that he'll say yes.

Question

Why would anyone pay an amount of money higher than the sticker price?
People will pay more when they perceive some type of benefit for themselves. Price can be important in the buying equation, but your customers will make a more expensive purchase if they feel that the value merits it.

Other Buyer Motivations

Some buyers are what are known as early adopters and love to have the newest gadgets or products. They are motivated by the excitement they get from being among the first to try a new technology. They may have a little of the creative inventor's mind, wanting to test out new gadgets as soon as possible. These are the buyers who bought the first car phones for five-figure sums or who spent six figures to buy jumbo TV screens when they first came out. These people are early adopters.

Some people's motivation is to do something new or different that sets them apart. They seek to create their own looks or trends. You see this desire often in Generation X in music and technology gadgets. These buyers are motivated to buy when they find something unique and different.

Some people will buy products and services that have a history of solving a specific problem. In products, they're looking for things with a reputation for being reliable. Their motivation is getting something that works and will keep working for a long time to come.

When this buyer is looking for services, he's looking for a seasoned professional who provides reliable, consistent work.

Using Motivations to Attract Customers

Find different ways that your product or service can save time for your customers. In addition, look for what you can do as a sales rep to save time for your prospect or customer. You personally become the added value behind a product, and that may be the motivator for someone buying your product or service.

How can your product or service save your customer money? Think in terms of both short-term and long-term savings. Compare the savings your customer could enjoy if she uses your product instead of that of a competitor. Point out concrete examples of the money the customer can save.

E ssential

> People will buy if you match them up with the perfect benefit of using your product or service. The key is determining which benefit motivates your customer. The primary buying benefits are price, quality, prestige, credibility, convenience, saving time, saving money, being easy to understand, being easy to use, setting trends, and enjoying the buying experience.

The easier your products or services are to use and understand, the more people will want to buy them. Your buyers are bombarded with information and don't have time to digest it all. Think what you can do to make it easier for your customer to understand your product. For example, if your product comes unassembled in a box and must be put together by the customer, go over the directions with him or give him your cell phone number to call for help if he has difficulty assembling it once he gets it home.

Buyer Motivational Benefits

Buyers feel they are getting a good deal if they perceive that the price is fair for the benefits they get from the product. They feel they're getting value for the price. Some buyers would rather buy fewer things but get superior quality in what they do buy. The socioeconomic differences have blurred in the last several years. Where once only the wealthy patronized certain high-end stores and bought certain luxury items, now other socioeconomic groups are finding ways to stretch their budgets to buy these same items when they want them.

Honing In on Trends

Some people buy something simply because it is the thing to do within their sphere of friends, coworkers, or competitors. This is a huge motivator for Generation Y. They first made the iPod popular. Then the trend of purchasing personal MP3 players spread to Gen X and baby boomers who liked to work out. And iPods are becoming increasingly popular with wider audiences of all generations as podcasting becomes more accessible and free.

Podcasts are recordings (similar to radio shows) that are downloadable from the Internet. They don't require a lot of effort or money to produce—anyone with something to say can create a podcast and post it for others to listen to. Podcasts are an excellent marketing tool for sales reps. They act as a relationship builder between you and the segment of your market that's tuned into the latest trends.

Credibility

People are often willing to pay more money for a product they know is durable or that comes from a company with a credible reputation. Credibility is established through experience—either personal experience with a company or product or secondhand experience (hearing about it from friends or acquaintances). That's a key reason word of mouth is so powerful. People want a product that is reliable and a service they can count on to provide results.

Time Savers

Everyone is busy with their lives—dealing with family, friends, work, apartments or houses, groceries, and everything else can make people feel like there isn't enough time in the day to get everything done. So products and services that make our lives more convenient will often win out, even if they are not the best quality. Getting something fast is more important sometimes than getting something perfect.

Because people are busy, they are always looking for ways to save time. This is a big buying motivator for many people. Just think of what you would or could do if you had an extra hour or two a day. How much are you willing to pay to get this extra time? You cannot afford *not* to delegate and hire out certain tasks if you want to spend quality time with your children or significant other, or free up time for yourself to exercise, devote to hobbies, and de-stress. Delegation means greater efficiency at work so you can also increase your work time and income by delegating.

Most people love a deal, no matter how much money they may have. Some individuals are so tempted by good deals that they purchase products or services they wind up never using, such as exercise equipment, TiVo, and clothes—just because they couldn't resist the deal!

Again, the idea is to make it as easy for your buyer to understand and use what you are selling. Most people don't want to take the time it would take to figure out something by themselves. One reason Apple computers sold so well when they were introduced in 1984 is because they were so easy to use. They didn't require anything to be put together, and—unlike other computers of the time—they could be run with almost no help from the instruction manual. The easier you can make it for people to use your product, the greater motivation they'll have to buy it.

Don't ignore the early adopter's market. Many consumers love the feeling of being out front, and not just in technology. There are early adopters for new restaurants, clothing styles, books, almost everything. Trendsetters have their antennae up for the next new thing, and at some point their usage tips the scale and results in more and more people buying the product or service. A major trend is making things swift and easy for these customers to help get your product in the hands of the people who will set the trends.

People will buy just for the experience. Fancy packaging such as the very recognizable Tiffany's box, an atmosphere like that of Starbucks or one of the new wine bars, a high level of customer service—all of these things create an experience for the customer that can motivate them to buy.

Alert

Any product or service that has earned a reputation for being good has a more flexible price point. People will pay more for a product or service that stands the test of time. It is your responsibility as the sales rep to help develop and communicate the credibility of your product by servicing your clients well.

This experience motivator is intangible in many ways. When you think of a coffeehouse that charges $3 and more for a cup of coffee, you know that the customer is not buying just coffee, but an entire experience. The experience may be an opportunity to unwind, for instance, or the ability to work on their laptop in a pleasant spot for a couple hours.

Price and Quality

The quality, prestige, or convenience of a product or service is often reflected in its price. As mentioned earlier, some hybrid cars are in such high demand that they're selling for $4,000 *over* the sticker price. Why? Because the dealers can get that price from their customers. Buyers who don't want to wait months to get a hybrid car (until demand and price go down) are willing to pay the premium.

You need to decide if your prospect or customer is more focused on price or quality. In other words, will he pay a premium for the perceived quality? As you help your prospects and customers decide which product or service is best for their needs and wants, you must pay attention to how important price and quality are to them. Look at the psychographics of the generations again to see what benefits will appeal to each segment of the population. Gen X-ers and Y-ers are most interested in price than some other generational groups, because they are just starting out in their first jobs at the beginning of their careers and aren't making a lot of money. Baby boomers, for the most part, are interested in price, but that price needs to come with a perceived value before they will buy. The baby boomers who have children living at home are the ones most interested in the price and quality of the products they purchase and in services that will preserve their time and energy. Seniors are very conscious of price compared to perceived value. Many of them are stunned by the way prices have increased compared to years ago.

People Buy Benefits, Not Features

When your prospects think about purchasing your products or services, they wonder how it will help *them*. Again, it comes down to the customer's perceived benefit, as she wonders, "What's in it for me?" The more you listen to what your prospect wants and needs, the more successful you will be in your selling career. The interesting thing is that most prospects and customers will tell you exactly what they need and want. However, many salespeople are primarily focused on their selling spiel and are not really listening. Listen carefully not only to what your prospects say but also the way they say it—what do they really feel they need and want? There are many common benefits buyers look for. They want a product that:

- Saves money
- Enhances sexuality
- Makes them look younger
- Improves their health
- Makes them look fitter
- Helps them lose weight
- Saves time

- Gives them a good experience
- Involves responsible marketing
- Has values consistent with theirs
- Makes them look smarter
- Increases self-esteem
- Increase their credibility
- Increases their popularity
- Makes them feel more powerful

Stay consciously tuned-in to these buyer benefits. Use these benefits to communicate to your prospects and customers what they can get out of your product or service.

Increase Buyer Desire

There is a great deal of information out there that can help you and boost your sales career by teaching you how to increase buyer desire. You can learn these tricks of the trade through books, online research, seminars, or simply by observing successful sales reps at their craft. Some of the most popular ways to increase a prospect's desire to buy include giving potential buyers a deadline, making them feel that they are part of an exclusive purchasing group, letting them know there is a limited supply of the product, offering bonuses, and making sure they understand the product or service.

Deadlines and Exclusivity

When you pose a deadline, you are telling your customer that there is a need for urgency in purchasing. A deadline means "You better hurry to purchase this product or service or you'll miss out on a great deal." This works equally well for a service as it does for a product. Gift certificates with expiration dates are great for creating this type of urgency.

As long as people are driven by their egos, they will respond well to the idea of being part of an exclusive group. Whether it's a club that can be joined by invitation only or a presale that's open only to VIPs, creating this air of exclusivity increases the desire to buy, because it makes the customer feel special.

Limited Supply and Bonuses

A limited supply implies a deadline—and, like a deadline, it means there's a need for urgency in purchasing. Telling customers that you have a limited supply alerts them to "buy before we run out!" For instance, if only the first fifty people who respond to an ad get the bargain rate, many prospects will buy at once. A limited supply also symbolizes a special deal, impressing upon customers a need to hurry to buy while quantities last.

People love to get things for free. You can find a wealth of bonuses in online marketing. For example, there are a number of educational or entertainment programs you can buy for only $39.95 with a handful of bonuses, such as additional CDs, DVDs, or accompanying printed materials.

Clear Understanding

If the prospect thinks that the product or service is too difficult or time-consuming to use, she'll more than likely choose not to purchase it. Make the directions or instructions that come with your product or service simple enough for a preteen to grasp easily. This will help ensure that people of various backgrounds will understand how to use your product, see that it's simple enough to implement, and ultimately think it is worth using to reap some sort of reward.

Added Value

As noted in previous chapters, price and quality are important. However, if you add value to your product or service, it will help make the price that much more palatable. There are several things you as the sales rep can add to the buying experience. Many women prefer to shop at dress boutiques where they get individual attention and help from salespeople during the buying process. Buying becomes a pleasant experience, with the salesperson showing a knowledge of and concern for the customer, as opposed to a frustrating trip to a large department store where clothes are in disarray and it's hard to find a salesperson to answer a question. Buyers are willing to pay higher prices in exchange for receiving this level of service. The service itself is a value that is added on top of the product that is for sale.

Alert

Provide the experience and people will buy. For example, spas started selling their plush bedding and fluffy robes when customers asked for them. Hotels took notice and introduced comfortable bedding and plush robes for sale as well. If you offer your customers a great experience, they will ask for more and pay more in exchange.

Make it convenient to use or purchase your product or service not just at the time of the sale but later on as well. One reason hybrid cars are selling so well is that in some states hybrid cars are allowed in the HOV lanes with only one passenger. It is convenient and saves time. The hybrid touches on three added-value benefits:

- It saves the driver time in commuting.
- It saves money on fuel.
- It is a socially responsible vehicle to drive.

Being socially responsible in itself triggers the feeling of prestige in some buyers. The other benefits, combined with the benefit of being socially responsible, make customers willing to wait weeks or months for the product and pay more to own it.

Follow-up is a huge added value that you can provide your prospects and customers no matter what field you're in. Customers often buy when a sales rep follows up with them. They are busy and appreciate any help they can get from the salesperson. They may have been intending to buy, but time got away from them, other tasks got in the way, and they hadn't had a chance to pursue it again. The sales rep who follows up and gets in touch with them will get the sale, because he makes it less work for the customer to make the purchase.

Buyers love guarantees because they provide a layer of security in case things go wrong with the product or service, or the customer finds that he did not make a good decision. If you provide a guarantee, be sure that fact is well-known among your customers. A guarantee is useless if no one knows about it.

It is important to be knowledgeable and to be nice. You might think that these two sales qualities are so basic that they don't need to be mentioned, but they do. The number of sales lost because sales professionals lack information about their wares or are dismissive toward customers is staggering.

Who Is Buying Now?

One reason to keep your finger on the pulse of your sales is to know who is buying and whether any shift in demographics has occurred. Sometimes a younger generation starts a trend but it is picked up later by their parents or the generation ahead of them. Items that were once considered a luxury have now become a necessity, even among people at lower income levels.

E ssential

Pay attention to consumer buying habits. You will become an expert in understanding your product's benefits as a result. An excellent marketing strategy is to routinely ask your customers what the main benefit was that motivated them to buy your products or services. Write it down, memorize it, and use this valuable feedback to sell to even more people.

People love to buy. Why? Because when a sales rep matches product and service benefits to a customer's needs and wants, it's fun.

Know whether the buyer is focused more on price or quality, and sell the benefits, not the features. Increase buyer desire by using deadlines, exclusivity, limited supply, bonuses, and clear understanding. Add value by providing a good experience, making it convenient, following up, highlighting guarantees, being knowledgeable and kind, and paying attention to who is buying today as opposed to yesterday.

Chapter 12

Who Are You to Your Customer?

Do your customers realize how your knowledge, experience, and products can help them? What defines you as "the" person to come to for your specific products or services? Your goal is to become so valuable to your customers that they feel they must work with you directly in order for their needs to be fully met. Selling yourself as a perceived value for your customers will generate increased profits and customer loyalty. If you can put yourself in the place of your prospects, you will be dialed into their needs.

Ways to Be Valuable

If it is possible, offer your customers a trial experience. Let customers try your service or product for a short time and before you start charging for it. By giving them time with your product or service, you are showing them your confidence in what you are selling. You also give them a chance to discover for themselves how great your product is.

Sales reps in every industry must stay focused on customers every step of the way and guide them through the potential pitfalls of the buying process. This is especially true in fields that involve significant complexity (and often very large amounts of money), such as in real estate, loans, investments, and remodeling of any type. Are you readily available to customers and do you return calls promptly? Or do your customers get irritated with your absence? You will know.

They may tell you directly or you may be able to pick up their frustration in their voices.

When you're speaking to your prospects or customers and you are truly hearing them and know you have met their needs and wants, then proceed as though you will be closing the deal. There are two reasons for this: The natural flow of customer service leads to closing the deal, and displaying confidence in the selling process helps close the sale.

As you share the major benefits of your product or service with your customers, watch their body language to pick up on which ones particularly hit home for them. As you continue to develop and build the relationship, keep emphasizing those benefits with your customers. It helps to keep them focused on how this product or service will be useful to them.

Identify Your Talents and Show Them

What are effective ways for you to show your talents to your prospects and customers? Showcasing your talents through exceptional customer service is just as important as making phone calls and paying personal visits. When your customers feel confident that you have their best interest at heart, they will trust you and will return to do business with you in the future.

How Thoughts Reflect

Psychological research reveals that people are composites of how they feel and think about events, people, or experiences. In other words, how you see yourself is expressed in how you behave toward others. If you don't feel like you're under the gun and you believe that you can do whatever you put your mind to, those two things work together to help motivate you to get things done without anxiety.

You may feel inspired by a motivational speech or a comment that resonates with you, and as a result you decide that you will make a change. This is an outside motivator. It's best to strive to find most of your motivation internally, with perhaps an occasional shot in the arm from external motivators.

External motivators are temporary, and internal motivators are more established and longer lasting. External motivators come from outside a person—from things such as seminars, conferences, and trophies or plaques awarded for good work. Internal motivators, however, are more sustaining because they come from within. These are things like having a strong feeling of confidence, knowing that you do good work for your customers, and having the desire to succeed.

Honing Personal Judgment Skills

Use your personal judgment skills to show your customers that you are confident and competent at your job, and that you believe in the product you are selling. Using personal judgment skills means trusting yourself to say the right thing, at the right time, in the right way. Personal judgment skills come from knowing your product inside and out, doing an accurate assessment of your prospect, and then answering directly how your product will link the two. You must let go of the traditional, more heavy-handed process of manipulation in sales, and trust your relationship with your customer. First, you must believe in yourself. Second, you must understand that the customer wants that degree of genuine connection. Third, you absolutely must practice. Sharp personal judgment skills come from the day-to-day experience of letting go of tactics and replacing them with outstanding customer service and awareness of your customer's needs.

Are You a Partner or a Pest?

Do you contact your customers only when you want them to buy something new or when they've gotten behind on their payments? If so, your customers could start to feel negative about your calls because their experience is that you contact them only because you want something from them. But if it's important to stay in contact (and it is!), you need a reason to call that isn't going to lead to negative feelings or feel like a waste of your customers' time.

If your business can provide the right information to prospects and customers, you'll have a valuable way to keep your customers interested in you and in your products and services. Keep in contact with your prospects and customers by sending them information on the products or services that they have purchased. This will help them to feel that you care about them (and what they're getting out of your product) instead of caring only about making the sale. Aftercare service is another form of added value you can bring to your customers.

Question

Why would a customer use you and not your competitor?
Customers will choose you because you have shown that you add value for them by being knowledgeable about your products or services, helping them solve a problem or improve a situation, exceeding their expectations, or giving them excellent customer service.

There are always things you can do to show your customers that you are a partner and not a pest. You can provide snippets of information that illuminate your industry and the ways it can benefit your customers' lives. What type of e-newsletter or blog can you create to communicate useful and informative material? Let your customers know of any special deals or price breaks you plan to offer on upcoming or new products or services. And make the purchase easy and convenient for your customers.

External and Internal Motivation

External motivation comes from outside your own emotions and feelings. People can find external motivation by listening to a motivational speaker, reading an inspirational quote, or watching an inspirational movie.

Many people attend wonderful motivational day seminars or multiday programs that leave them flying higher than a kite when they're over. But after a few days, the excitement wears off and the person loses steam, setting aside the materials and doing nothing. Or perhaps they do something different to effect change, but they don't keep it up for long.

Employee incentive programs are externally motivated. Incentive programs offer rewards of some type to employees who meet or exceed certain goals or milestones. Some employees are very responsive to this type of external motivation, and others are not. Because of the type of personality that is drawn to a career in sales, a higher percentage of sales reps is influenced by external motivation than is typical of employees in other industries.

When you develop an incentive program, be sure the external motivators are truly motivating your employees or customers. Think of external motivators as injections that generate activity and excitement when first administered but dissipate after a while in the bloodstream. You must keep providing external motivators to keep getting the same level of results.

Internal motivators are what keep a fire in your belly. Some of the ways to find internal motivation are by identifying what is really important to you as a person and how your career reflects that and by identifying how your values and your sales career merge. Do you reach your goals by living your values or by reading inspirational quotes that reflect your values, remind you of what's important, and help get you "back on track" again? Some activities that can provide you with a boost of internal motivation include writing new goals or rereading past goals, reducing stress and creating energy through exercise or listening to a motivational speaker, or finding a local role model whom you can connect with and model your career after.

Traits of a Professional

It can be disheartening to be around people who are constantly late or half asleep, who show only half-hearted interest (at best) in their work, who have nothing interesting to say, or who refuse to listen to what a customer wants but pushes him to buy something he really doesn't want.

Falling into a Rut

It may seem obvious that these attitudes bring people down, but many sales professionals get into ruts and run on autopilot. This can happen for any number of reasons. Some reasons are more dramatic than others—a breakup with a significant other or the discovery of a serious disease. Some are less dramatic, such as a feeling of boredom or sameness or of not going anywhere.

To be the best you can be for yourself and for your customers, it is vital that you focus on four things every day:

1. Promptness
2. Alertness
3. Being interesting
4. Listening

A professional understands the importance of being on time. You may even want to show up for meetings with prospects and clients five minutes earlier than planned. It shows that you consider your time with them important and shows that you respect your prospect's or customer's time. Your customers should be able to set their watches by your promptness.

Overstimulation

So much stimulation surrounds us in the form of sound, sight, and action that it can sometimes be hard to stay alert and focused. However, when you lose focus or you're not entirely "there," this comes across strongly to your customers in your body language. Your customers interpret this to mean that you don't want to be there with them or that their purchase is not important to you.

Turn off your cell phone when you are with your customers. Not only does it show courtesy to them but it also keeps your focus on their needs by eliminating a potential distraction. When your phone rings, even if you don't answer it, just the act of hearing it or looking at it can distract you and undermine your alertness.

Communicating Effectively

As you help your prospect, make sure you involve everyone in interesting conversation. Some sales reps are uncomfortable talking unless they are cracking jokes—bad jokes at best. If you aren't confident that you can get your ideas across well, if you feel at a loss for words too often or are uncomfortable communicating, make the effort to go to a Toastmasters meeting. This can help you learn how to communicate more effectively.

You know you can hear. The real trick is to listen to what the other person is telling you. If you listen, you'll be amazed at what you'll pick up from your prospects and customers.

Are You a Face, a Voice, or Cyberspace?

What is the main method you use to stay in contact with your customers? Is it with face-to-face meetings, with phone calls, or via e-mail? You may want to use a combination of all three types of communication rather than relying too heavily on only one method.

Meeting face-to-face is an excellent way to stay in contact, keep your relationship going strong, and find ways to help your customers with more products. However, this is also the most time-consuming way to stay in touch and may be more than is necessary in many instances.

Calling works very well for keeping in touch, and most customers like to hear your voice because it also helps to keep up the relationship bond. But again, using the telephone may be a time waster for you and your client, especially if you have trouble reaching each other and go back and forth with voice mail messages.

E ssential

You may want to use the 5:1:1 ratio—five e-mails for every phone or face-to-face contact. As long as you stay in contact with your prospects and customers often, they usually feel taken care of. If, however, you don't hear back after two e-mails, then call. Their e-mail may be down.

E-mail saves time and lets you avoid having to coordinate your busy schedule with theirs just to exchange information or ask questions. This works especially effectively with online purchasers.

However, it is always a good idea to give your customers another way to contact you just in case their e-mail is down temporarily.

If e-mail is the only stream of communication with your customer, there could be room for a disconnect, as there is no inflection of body language or tone of voice with e-mail. And if your e-mail is down, you miss the communication altogether.

Chapter 13

Marketing Is Your Sales Engine

Your car won't run without the engine working, and likewise your sales career will not improve on its own without alterations and regular maintenance to keep it on track and running smoothly and efficiently. If you don't maintain the marketing engine, your time and effort will not equal your profits, and you will end up losing money, customers, or both. This chapter gives you some creative insights into keeping your marketing engine working for you.

Developing Visual Aids

At conferences, evaluation forms are often distributed to participants after every speaker. One common question included on these evaluations asks audience members to rate the visual aids used in the speaker's presentation. Good visual aids are important. Why spend a lot of time developing a good speech, full of useful information, and then dampen the experience with poor (or no) visual aids? People remember things better if they experience it with multiple senses— both seeing and hearing information is important to retaining it.

A successful sales professional knows that the collateral material can help or hinder the speech. All of your collateral material should reinforce your image, brand, professionalism, and product or service focus. In other words, your business cards, stationery, postcards, Web site, blog, e-zines and advertising should use similar colors and fonts and include your unique tag line.

Longer Speeches

For speeches that last more than thirty minutes, always include handouts and a PowerPoint presentation. They will help hold the interest of your participants and give them something to focus on during longer presentations. They also benefit you by helping you to remember the key points you want to get across. All handouts should be informative and fun and interesting to look at, to ensure that they will be something the prospect or customer will want to keep.

Shorter Speeches and Teleseminars

A short speech is anything that lasts less than thirty minutes. You want to include handouts for short presentations as well. The key to successfully presenting a shorter speech is to focus on the ideas—the speech itself—with few if any PowerPoint slides.

Teleseminars are seminars given over the telephone while participants follow along with a PowerPoint presentation. Teleseminars are helpful tools that can make a very strong impact on your customers. The ideal length of time for a teleseminar is usually one hour, including a fifty-minute presentation and a ten-minute period at the end that is open for questions. While the speakers are talking, everyone else is on mute, so participants don't hear lots of excessive or distracting noises.

Meetings

For meetings you may want to include handouts and possibly a PowerPoint presentation, depending upon the amount of time you have and the purpose of the meeting. A good general rule is to include a PowerPoint presentation with about twenty slides if there are several people present in your meeting. If there are only one or two other people, a PowerPoint presentation is usually overkill.

Some speakers might use handouts with certain key words left off of them as aids to their presentations. This makes listeners follow along closely so they can fill in the blanks with the proper words. It helps to engage them in the presentation, which will help participants remember the essence of you, your personality, and your material. Handouts also give participants an easy place to take notes of your speech.

Trade Shows

Trade shows are excellent venues at which to present your products and services, and they are cost-effective, because you're able to reach a targeted group of people. You just have to identify what you want to say and how to say it. There are three important elements in creating a successful trade show exhibitor booth: Pay close attention to pre-event marketing, event marketing on the day of the convention, and post-event marketing.

Follow-up is essential for reaping the most from successful trade shows. Trade shows have a crescendo effect. You begin the selling process before the event during pre-event marketing by sending out postcards, writing e-mails, and making phone calls. At the show, attention and interest peak, and after the show you need to continue the momentum with follow-up marketing.

To generate interest before the event even starts, offer each person in your database a free gift for visiting your booth. On the day of the event, you can generate more traffic in your booth by offering something with a far-reaching aroma, such as popcorn. (People are usually hungry after walking around a trade show all day!) Have enough staff manning your booth so that all potential customers are greeted and offered help if they have questions. Ask for the business cards of the people who visit your booth, and then make the time to follow up with everyone who leaves a card. And be sure you look to see that each card has the person's e-mail address on it before he or she leaves your booth.

The Internet

The biggest and fastest growing area of marketing is found on the Internet. From Web sites to blogs to e-books and e-zines, the Internet offers a variety of possible advertising mediums in an easy-to-use package.

All sales reps should have an Internet presence that includes their own Web site. Web sites today are as important as phone numbers and e-mail addresses. Buy a domain name and use an e-mail address related to it, rather than using a free account like AOL or Yahoo! The more professional your e-mail address, the more credible you are to your prospect and customer. You can either develop your own Web site (there are numerous software programs that make it easy) or pay a service to develop one for you.

Getting Started

To get started creating your Web site, ask yourself, "What do I want it to accomplish?" Consider whether you want to use your Web site as your brochure, to sell products or services, to generate interactivity with clients, or a combination of all three. Then develop a site with clear goals in mind.

Just as a brochure does, your Web site shares information about you, your company, and its products and services. But your "brochure on the Web" can convey a lot more about you. It is also easier and less expensive to update than printed materials. One of the many wonderful things about having a Web site is that it sells for you 24/7. To take the greatest advantage of this huge benefit of having an online presence, install a software program on your site that allows users to purchase your products without your active participation whenever possible. This makes it possible for users to buy your product at anytime, day or night. Your Web site is also the perfect place to offer downloads of your seminars to anyone who was unable to attend or who wants a refresher on the material you covered.

Design Choices

Select the colors for your Web site carefully. Do a little research on colors and the psychological impact they can have on you and the visitors to your site. Ideally you should make them consistent with the colors of your letterhead and business cards. If your collateral material has no distinct colors or patterns, then simply choose the colors that your buyers will find appealing. Fonts also convey a great deal in a subtle way. You need to pay attention to what your chosen font says about you and about the products you are selling. Choosing an appropriate and design-friendly font is one area where an expert graphic designer can help you immeasurably.

Web sites are visual media. What kinds of pictures do you want to use? You can use images of real people or stock photos representing your products and services. Always include your logo and your tag line to tie in the Web site with your other business materials.

 Fact

Web site graphics are potent communications tools. Consumers are hooked on color and interesting graphics. Nowhere are these things more important than in advertising—and your Web site is advertising. Keep text to a minimum; your site should be interactive rather than just something to read. Interactive sites keep the prospect's attention longer.

Every word you write on your Web site must matter. Pay special attention to the main page of your Web site and the organizational tabs that allow people to move through the site. Make sure they are arranged logically and clearly and make it easy to navigate the different pages of the Web site.

Be sure your content includes key words used in your industry, especially on your main page. These key words allow popular search engines to find your Web site and display it for potential customers who are in the market for something you can sell them.

Blogs

A blog is a shortened term for a Weblog. Blogs are Web-based publications that feature articles, essays, and links posted chronologically on a regular basis. Many blogs give readers the capability to post comments on the page in response to postings, thus making it more interactive than a simple newsletter. In the business world blogs create a platform for keeping businesses in touch with their customers. They're a great way to help people remember you the next time they may need your products or services. You may also choose to launch a personal blog in addition to your business blog to give you even more ways to stay in touch and build relationships with your prospects and clients.

Blogs have become an important part of marketing plans for sales reps. They are most effective for communicating practical information about your products and services from a wide perspective.

Blogs work in many different ways. They can:

- Help you stay in contact with prospects and customers.
- Remind your prospects and customers about you regularly.
- Help you build a "virtual" relationship with your clients as you share information about you and your philosophies.
- Update your prospects and customers with new and useful information about your products or services and their benefits.

Blogs are spreading like wildfire. According to the *Wall Street Journal*, there were over 20 million of them by September 2005, and more than a 100 blog search engines like Technorati.com to help Internet users find the ones that suit their needs and interests.

E-Books

E-books are a wonderful way to start developing interest in your product and stand out from your competitors. Your prospects and clients will see you as more of an expert knowing that you have published a book or an e-book. People tend to think a person is more serious and committed and has more expertise in the field if she has written about it.

E-Zines

An e-zine is an online newsletter. There are excellent books and e-books on how to get the best results from a blog or an e-zine created to increase sales. E-zines are much more cost-effective and have a better read-through than traditional mailed newsletters. They are an excellent way to keep in touch with your prospects and customers, and they serve as an effective communication vehicle for promoting new products and services as well as for offering discounts.

Advertising

Advertising can produce excellent results, but it must be used consistently, be focused on a specific purpose, and be measured for return on investment. First, determine the top five advertising outlets that your target market reads, listens to, surfs, or watches. Do your homework and learn what the costs would be to advertise in those places on a regular basis. Advertising only works if it is consistent. People are bombarded by so many communications and attention-grabbers everywhere they go; one or two exposures to an ad will not sink in. It usually takes about seven reminders before a prospect thinks of using you to solve his problem.

Another reason to develop a consistent marketing program is so that your picture or name and product penetrates people's "awareness" seven different times. You may want to call, send them a thank-you note, write an e-mail, send a postcard, send them an e-zine, and advertise in a targeted paper or on radio station that they read or listen to. You must be persistent and consistent.

With print advertising, it is not necessary even when you're first starting out to advertise every day or even every week. Committing to advertising in a circular every other week can be enough.

The least expensive and most effective print advertising is the business card. One of the first things you should do when you first meet someone is hand her your business card. It should include your name, business address, e-mail and Web site addresses, phone number, and fax number. It is also a good idea to include your tag line.

Everything about your business card should reinforce the image and the brand you are projecting. Raised lettering on your business card is still considered the gold-standard for sales reps and offers a subtle expression of professionalism. The difference in cost between

1,000 homemade laser cards and raised lettering cards is small, especially when you consider the power of professional-looking business cards that have raised lettering.

Alert

If you are in an industry in which it is common to include a photo of yourself on your business cards, have the picture taken by a professional photographer. Look as natural as possible; you want people to recognize you in person just from seeing your photo.

Your print advertising campaign may include mailers. Prospects are bombarded by lots of postcards, ads, and other collateral material in their mail and e-mail boxes every day, so you must get their attention with a grabber headline. This grabber is similar to a press release headline that gets the attention of media.

It's important to set up a budget for advertising and use it as creatively as you can. Do not depend on print advertising as your sole marketing tool to find your prospects. It can be expensive and should be only one strategy in your marketing tool kit.

Creative Press Releases

A press release can be an invaluable asset to your marketing chest of tools. There are two important elements about a press release that will be picked up by the media: the headline and the story angle. The headline needs to capture the attention of an editor or producer. Look at magazine and newspaper headlines to see how they capture interest and leave you wanting to know more. Additionally, the content of the press release should be about something other than just you and your business. If your press release feels or reads like you're just promoting your business, it will be tossed like a hot potato. To get noticed, write a press release about an issue related to your industry, product, or service or one that announces a new product or service and its benefits. You also want to include in the body of the press release the answers to those five important questions:

- Who?
- What?
- Where?
- When?
- Why?

Include your contact information on the top right-hand side of the press release.

Always send your press releases to people and businesses in your database as well as to the media outlets you've chosen. You want your prospects and customers to know about what you are doing, any changes going on in your industry, or anything new that is available. Plus, it is an excellent way to keep your name in front of your next buyer!

Your Service and Professionalism

Customer service is actually a marketing tool. It is an area where great sales reps can set themselves apart from their competitors, because quality customer service is rare. Create a list of what areas of customer service you have developed to provide an above-average experience for your prospects and customers. This customer service checklist may include such items as:

- Giving information and providing service in a timely manner.
- Following through on promises
- Sending customers articles or Web site information about areas related to your product or service

By sending your customers helpful information, you make them feel that you want to help them and make their buying experience convenient. Establishing a high level of customer service—and becoming known for it—will generate leads better than any other advertising medium can.

E ssential

If you got your prospect's e-mail address at your first meeting (as you should have), respond to him by e-mail when appropriate. Make sure you leave a message in your voice mail for callers, asking them to be as specific as possible when leaving messages so you can get the information they're looking for sooner. Your receptionist or voice mail message should ask callers to leave their phone numbers and e-mail addresses to make it as quick as possible for you to get back to them. Keep track of the types of questions your customers are calling about; you probably receive many calls from customers simply looking for updates. The prospect or customer wants to know where you are in the deliverables process, ask a quick question about using the products or services, or perhaps order an accessory. The high-performing sales rep documents these questions so that she can include answers to common questions in the selling process, have replies prepared to send out via e-mail for the top ten or twelve questions, or perhaps train an assistant to follow up and answer certain types of questions.

Partner with your customers—your job all along the way is to partner with your prospects or customers to help solve their problems or needs. The more your customers feel that you are in this together with them and that you truly care, the more your sales will increase and the more word-of-mouth advertising you'll get—the best kind in the world!

Too many professionals lose all the momentum of the sale because they forget to follow up or, worse, they don't think it's necessary. Other than having the customer sign the contract and building the relationship, follow-up is your most important concern.

Show How You Are Unique

Your appearance is the first thing your prospects and customers notice, and your appearance is uniquely you. Prospects tend to remember sales reps who dress appropriately for the industry they're in. There is a psychological reason for this. People like to put people into nice neat categories that fit with their expectations of a particular person, group, or industry. Dress according to your profession and keep it professional. If you sell resort properties you may not wear a suit, but if you are selling financial services to serious investors, you probably will.

Whether it's fair or not, how you look and the way you speak are critical to making a good impression, particularly at the first meeting. It is estimated that you have approximately thirty seconds to make a good impression when you first meet someone.

Your appearance makes the first impression about your professionalism. And the first thirty seconds of your introduction or conversation makes the second. Your appearance is one more way you can subliminally reinforce how well you do your job and your level of professionalism. This is especially crucial when meeting a prospect for the first time. Your first impression can either help or hurt a sale. Successful sales reps use this knowledge to their benefit.

Show How Your Products or Services Are Unique

The more you can get your prospects or customers to engage and interact with your products and services, the greater the chance of selling to them. Show how unique your products and services are. Offer free samples or free trials so they can experience how it benefits them. If this isn't possible, use an interactive approach such as showing a PowerPoint presentation, photos, or video of others using the product or service in different places, cultures, and locales. Many stores and showrooms use this method of selling, with a variety of computer and TV screens running constantly showing examples of the product in use, which they hope will inspire customers to want to use it, too.

Question

What type of video should I create?
Present the different uses of your product and show previous customers using your products and giving testimonials. Tie it in with your other marketing using the same logo, tag line, and image. Be sure to include spoken information about the product, too. (Not everyone will watch every second, but if they hear it, they'll still get the message.)

Free samples are the ultimate in show-and-tell. Gift certificates (that include expiration dates!) for an hour of free consulting or a miniature version of your product can be great marketing tools. If you are in the food business, free samples are definitely the best marketing tool you have in your arsenal. Debbi Fields, who started the wildly successful cookie company called Mrs. Fields, gave away more cookies than she sold when she first started. Costco uses this same approach of giving out free samples to sell some of its food products and to create an experience for shoppers.

Showing, Not Telling

The old cliché that a picture is worth a thousand words is certainly true in the marketing world. It's important to use photos of yourself, your customers, and your products in your marketing. Place them on your Web site, in your presentations, and on your handouts. It is most beneficial to have visuals that show people using the products and that provide an interactive feel.

A powerful way to show your prospect or customer your products or services is to "live it." There is no better seal of approval than personally using the products and services you're selling. Sales professionals at clothing stores often wear clothes sold at the store. Some businesses require their sales reps to wear shirts or jackets that feature the company name and logo. You need to live the culture, drive the car, eat the food, speak the language.

Creative Engagement

Aroma has a powerful and often subtle appeal that reaches deep inside people. Think of the smell of hot bread in a bakery, warm cashew nuts on the street, or coffee in a café. Auto buyers speak of the "new-car smell" as a great pleasure of driving a new car. Some banks pipe the scent of vanilla through their air-conditioning systems to calm waiting customers, and retailers of beds use lavender scents to boost sales.

Be careful, though, about the scents you use. Aroma can have a powerful positive effect, but the wrong scent can have a negative impact. Many scents, especially floral scents, can trigger allergic reactions or can give people headaches. As you begin to use scents you will become used to them and may have a tendency to use too much without realizing it. Aroma must be subtle and enticing without any negative reactions to be effective.

A tantalizing aroma can be especially important in trade show booths, when you have literally only a few seconds to attract people walking by. You may want to pop popcorn or dip apples in caramel to offer to visitors at your trade show booth. Aroma helps bring prospects and clients to you, thereby giving you more opportunities to sell.

Ask for and Use Testimonial Letters

Ask for testimonials while the coals are hot. You do not have to wait until the sale is completed. Write the testimonials for clients using the words they have used to describe their satisfaction with you and your products or services and have them sign them. You'll get more testimonials this way than if you wait for customers to write them themselves, no matter how good their intentions may be.

Testimonial letters are important to your selling career because they work to bolster your credibility. You can use them for years in many different areas of marketing your business. Use them on your brochures, Web site, advertisement, e-book, books, workbooks, and trade show fliers.

Alert

Don't consider a sale to be "the end." Take the long view and consider your selling relationship with each customer as never ending. You'll stay in contact with the people in your database knowing that there are always more products or services to sell. Plus, you never know when a customer may suddenly decide to buy after saying no at first.

Brainstorm Regularly to Create New Ideas

Do you ever find yourself in the middle of a meal when suddenly a great idea comes to you out of the blue? With informal brainstorming a rush of ideas can occur when you least expect it: over meals, chatting on the phone, taking a shower, at a party, or taking a morning walk.

Formal brainstorming is planned but can lead to just as great insights and ideas. There is only one rule that's necessary in a formal brainstorming session: No one criticizes, critiques, or laughs at anyone else's ideas. A brainstorming session should be a place for completely free and open discourse, an environment that leads to lots of creative ideas. This is what makes brainstorming such a fruitful exercise.

You may have great luck in brainstorming with your clients, or you may want to brainstorm with colleagues or friends first for ideas to present to clients. Brainstorming works best in a group format, since an idea from one person can trigger totally different ideas in others.

Plan brainstorming sessions with your team on a monthly basis. Include your prospects and customers, vendors, and anyone else you feel is important for your sales team. You will receive invaluable information and ideas.

Chapter 14

Finding the Yes Factor

The key word in sales is yes. The remarkable thing about the yes factor is that it works two ways. When the sales professional is able to say yes, prospects and customers find it easy to say yes as well. This chapter discusses several effective options to help implement the yes factor. If you can eliminate the downside for your prospects and customers by allowing them to try your products and services for free, you have made it easier for them to say "yes." Add a no-risk guarantee to your offer, and watch your sales go up.

Getting Your Customer to Yes

Prospects and customers can easily be overwhelmed by the flood of advertising, product and service options, Web sites, podcasts, and blogs that are out there competing for their attention. This competition presents one more reason to fuel and refuel your brand, keep products and service information updated, and stay current with trends in your field, as well as those in other industries. You never know when or where you'll find an idea that you can adapt to use with your prospects and clients. Offering your prospect or customer a tailor-made twist on the no-risk guarantee is part of the yes factor.

Observing Trends

The key to any sale is for the prospect to become a customer and for the existing customer to keep purchasing your products and services by saying yes to you. By observing consumer trends you can learn a wealth of demographic and psychographic information about what and why various groups are buying. Be aware of these trends both in your own industry and others. Customize and use those ideas to make it easier for your prospects and customers to say yes.

Getting to yes means getting your customer interested in your product or service. One way to do this is to get him to try it out. No matter what your industry, you can likely find some way to encourage prospects to try what you're selling. For example, consider a local transit board that's trying to increase ridership on city buses. It may choose to offer packaged day trips to local events. The program persuades people who do not normally use public transit to travel to these events on by bus. As a result they see how easy and convenient it is to use and may be more likely to consider using one of the regular transit routes the next time they go out.

Free Services or Items

Another example of companies making it easy for their customers to say yes is the increasingly popular trend of offering free shipping with a minimum purchase amount, which motivates consumers to buy more products. How can you bring extra value to your customers and still maintain a healthy profit? Notice that the free shipping is given *with a minimum order.* You do the math!

Offering a free trial period is another way you can help your customer get to yes. Free trials give customers a chance to see for themselves how they like the product or service, with no cost to them. An example is the *Wall Street Journal*, which offers a free subscription to its online site for two full weeks. Readers have the opportunity to try the online version without making a purchase first.

If you're a service consultant, why not offer a complimentary session for your prospects and customers? You could offer a free session of telecoaching (coaching a group of people over the phone), a free teleseminar (a seminar hosted on a conference call), or a free Webinar (a seminar hosted over the Internet). The information you provide is a "free sample," which helps eliminate the risk to the customer (it costs them nothing) and gets you closer to the yes factor.

Question

Banks are in stiff competition with other financial companies to sign up consumers for their products. Part of the reason Washington Mutual may have grown so rapidly is that many of its bank branches act and look more like retail stores than banks, with customer service at the front line. "Concierges" walk customers to different areas of the bank, depending on whether they are looking for loans, investments, or other banking products. The branches also sell software to help customers with financial planning and offer treats like chocolates and coffee. All these service-oriented pieces help the bank's customer see the positive side, or yes factor, of doing business with Washington Mutual as opposed to another bank.

Many businesses offer free shipping for holiday purchases. A survey conducted by Shop.org and BizRate Research showed that 79 percent of online retailers offered free shipping as long as the customer purchased a minimum amount. Many consumers mistakenly think that freight is a profit source for companies, but the reality is that offering free shipping chips away at the bottom line of the company. It truly is a money-saving value for the consumer, and a way for the company to get buyers to the yes factor.

Building a Strong Team

Teamwork matters. It takes a whole team of people to make a customer happy. Your team may include the manufacturer, the vendor, someone in the warehouse, people who are centers of influence in your targeted groups, and mentors. Find the team that works best for you and nurture it. The team you put together does matter and the support you get from them are all part of the yes factor.

The Value of Strong Teams

Teamwork can make the difference between life and death, as mounting research from businesses and hospitals suggests. Two professors from the Harvard Business School, Robert Huckman and Gary Pisano, analyzed Pennsylvania heart surgeons who routinely practiced at more than one hospital. According to the *Wall Street Journal,* the professors found that "the death rates from similar procedures performed by the same surgeon can vary as much as fivefold at different hospitals. Most of the time, patients did better in the hospital where their surgeon performed more operations." The implication is that outcomes are better when surgeons are working with a team working at peak performance. Two other Harvard professors found similar teamwork results on Wall Street, where a team approach to productivity worked better than focusing on individual "star" producers.

Addressing Your Needs

What kind of team do you need? A realtor may want an assistant who follows up with paperwork and manages e-mail and calls, another team member to keep contact management up-to-date, another to create the graphics for postcards and Web sites, and still another to manage the Web site content and other material that needs to stay fresh. Your team members do not have to be full-time employees. They may be independent freelancers who offer quick turnaround, are productive, and inspire trust.

You may feel you don't have enough money to hire such a team, but high-producing sales professionals recognize a crucial point about their industry: The business tasks that keep you from focusing on the activities you excel at, such as dealing directly with prospects and customers, creating the vision, and "working" the contacts, should be delegated to other professionals. The more time you have to focus on what you do best your business, the more successful you will be.

E ssential

The most successful sales professionals are those who spend the most time servicing their customers and who take time to plan their marketing strategies on a consistent basis. The majority of time should be spent working on your business. Develop and plan your marketing and selling strategies and systems, so that your business runs smoothly. Automate any areas that you can, such as the timing of and methods by which your prospects and customers receive information, gifts, or discounts.

By building a strong team, you and your prospects and customers are creating the yes factor. Someone on your team is helping to build or maintain the relationship with your customer, and your customer is realizing the integrity and attentiveness of your whole team. When a prospect or customer knows that there is someone on the team to take care of him and his needs, that helps him say yes to you.

What Happens If They Don't Buy

You can't expect to sell to every person every time, no matter how well you screen your prospects or how excited a customer may have been about your product. Sometimes things happen that you have no control over. Perhaps the prospect really never had any intent to buy. Perhaps this was her first attempt to get a feel for what's available and compare products and she wasn't ready to purchase. There are many other factors you have no control over, but if your prospect doesn't buy this time, no matter what the reason, do two important things: First, record the questions she asked and your answers to them in a journal or database. Remember to include her age (guess, if you have to) and anything else you learned about her during the process. You will find it helpful to see the trends that emerge. You may find that a certain demographic group buys less often than another, or that males shopping by themselves buy twice as often as females shopping by themselves. As a beginning sales rep, these observations will help you get a better handle on how and where to make changes in your sales protocol. As a seasoned sales professional, you will be able to use this information to target your prospects and customers even better.

Second, remember that you are responsible for the way you communicate and deal with people. The critical point here is that you must always concentrate on developing the relationship, because that is what selling really is.

Picking Up on Nonverbal Communication

Your prospects will tell you exactly what they need and want, if you allow them the time and courtesy to communicate. Your job is multifold—to listen to what they say and how they say it. The more you listen and focus, the more you will hear "yes."

You can do this best by focusing on your prospects' and clients' verbal and nonverbal communication.

Here's an interesting thing about verbal communication: The words spoken are not always a good indicator of what prospects or customers want. The main reason is that they may not really know *why* they want a product or service. A customer may say she wants to save time but, by asking open-ended questions, you may learn that this single mother is tired at the end of the day and feels guilty about the scant time and energy she has left for her children.

Much of selling is psychology. You don't have to be a psychologist to be a high producer, but some tips can help you communicate better with your prospects and customers. You experience nonverbal communication in your life every day. A person's body language—the way he picks up his phone when it rings, the look on his face, how fidgety he is—shows whether he is in a good or bad mood or whether he feels pressed for time. If what a person says (verbal communication) conflicts with how he says it (nonverbal communication), ask questions to clarify the inconsistency. When spoken language differs from body language, people are more likely believe the body language. It takes far less time to clarify someone's meaning upfront than it does to repair the damage miscommunication can create.

 Fact

You can often "read" your prospects or customers by their body language. For example, if they say they are interested in a particular product but their voice inflection and facial expressions show otherwise, go back to square one. Make sure you ask the right open-ended questions, listen, and watch how they answer.

Body language to watch is voice inflection, the position of the person's arms and eyes, and whether he is shifting positions and postures. The pitch of a person's voice rises when she gets excited, which can be a good or bad thing. A low, soft voice may indicate either a lack of interest or shyness. (As you build a relationship with the prospect, you'll be better able to tell the difference.)

Crossed arms usually indicate that the person is either cold or resistant to your ideas. The more eye contact you have, the better you can connect with the other person. While there are several cultures where eye contact is frowned upon, the American culture is not one of them. If your customer is looking away from you and not directly into your face or at what you are showing them, they may be revealing either low self-confidence or a lack of interest in you or your product or service.

Body language is sometimes more honest than the actual words. For example, when someone is telling you a lie or is uncomfortable with what he is saying, you will often find that he shifts position, scratches his head, or fidgets. Unconsciously, people communicate most clearly and honestly through their body language. Learn to read what they're telling you.

Becoming Familiar with Consumer Trends

Understanding the trends in other fields, related or not, opens up new opportunities in operations, marketing, identifying new markets, and so much more. Here are a few trends that may inspire you to try a new kind of marketing and open up your creative mind.

Ski Resorts

More baby boomers are skiing. Ski resorts know that if they keep their trails groomed, they will attract more people from this age group, because aging boomers are less likely to get hurt or put undue stress on their bodies if they are skiing on smooth, well-kept snow. Because of the increase in the number of senior skiers, several resorts stopped offering free skiing to people over seventy, because they found that they could still attract plenty of older skiers who were willing to pay the lift ticket prices. According to the National Ski Areas Association, skiers age forty-five or older have increased from 21 percent of total skiers during the 1997–1998 ski season to 31 percent in the 2005–2006 season.

Some resorts have found even more ways to cater to the baby boomer skiers. Aspen Mountain, for example, offers a "Bumps for Boomers" program that teaches skiers how to go from groomed slopes to more difficult terrain.

Other resorts are seeking to attract a younger and more aggressive type of winter athlete: the snowboarder. They are creating dedicated snowboard runs, so that snowboarders can snowboard without interference from downhill skiers and the chance of injuries from collisions will decrease.

Magazines

Reader's Digest recognizes that many of its readers are older and, in an effort to target these readers, publishes a boomer-senior version of the magazine with larger print for aging eyes. Companies whose major target groups are older baby boomers and seniors might be wise to have a large-print version of their printed material so this group can read the "fine print" better. It's another nonverbal way for the sales professional to say, "Trust me. I'm trying to serve you better."

This reflects the trend of tailoring a magazine to a specific reader through special features.

A recent trend in magazine advertising is to include testimonials and pictures of "real" people, usually with information like their age and what they do for a living. A reason for the increasing popularity of this trend is that people are looking for something "real." Banks often use billboards that show a real person using their banking services. One women's retail clothing store printed a full-page color ad in a national publication showing real sales associates who worked at the store. An ad for a hygiene product featured real women who were not model-thin sharing how much they enjoyed using the product. You can be sure that you will start to see this type of "real advertising" more and more. This has become an effective consumer marketing trend that you could potentially adopt in your business to boost your sales.

Beer and Wine

Baby boomers have favored wine over beer and cocktails in a big way, whereas Generations X and Y women are moving toward the low-carb cocktail. Older members of Generation Y, or the echo boomers (ages 21 to 28) as they are sometimes called, are going the cocktail route as well, probably because of the image of sophistication the hard alcohol industry has spent millions of dollars projecting. This is an example of a trend that reflects marketing. Younger generations have been swayed by advertising that depicts an air of sophistication that comes with consuming cocktails like martinis and cosmopolitans. In your sales career, you can capitalize on trends in marketing to sell your product to an appropriate demographic so that your chances of getting them to say yes to your product are greater.

Listening to What Your Prospect Wants

Listen in depth to learn the true needs of your prospects and customers. They may say they want a security system, but what they really want is peace of mind—the assurance that no one will sneak in through a window at night and snatch their child. You might give tips on ways to keep children protected in the house during the day when an adult is not home and how to make the windows more secure.

If you're a sales rep for a beauty aid, find out what your prospects and customers want most. Of course they want to look good, but do they fear getting older and imagine that they are becoming unattractive to potential romantic partners? Perhaps they seek to remarry and want to meet their special partner. You would tailor their products to address those needs. By really listening and asking questions, you can service your prospects and customers better and, as a result, make multiple sales to each customer.

Using Open-Ended Questions

Open-ended questions help you to start a real dialogue with your prospects and customers. An open-ended question is one that cannot be answered by a simple yes or no or by a limited statement of fact. Closed-ended questions—such as "What is your age?" and "Where do you live?"—aim for specific, well-defined answers. If selling is about relationship building, then you want to ask many open-ended questions. Letting your customer speak freely gives you more information.

Here are some questions that work well for many sales professionals:

- "How can I help you best?"
- "What is most important to you regarding your insurance needs [your marketing needs, or whatever is being sold]?"
- "What is most important to you about working with your employees?"
- "If money weren't an issue, what product or service would you most like to have?"
- "What is it about this product or service that you like most?"

These examples give you an idea of the types of questions that can get your prospect or customer talking about what matters. Talking this way deepens your relationships with prospects and customers. It inspired their trust, and they will share their honest desires.

Winning the Word-of-Mouth Game

The world has become a much smaller place as it has become easier and easier to move people and goods across vast distances in a short time. In any large city around the world you'll find a melting pot of different cultures, languages, and economies.

To tap into the global market while paying attention to local and regional markets is to be sensitive to other cultures and include them in your marketing efforts. If you are presently selling to another country, you can include real people from that country in your advertising or you can use their language to say, "I like it, it works," or something similar to let other consumers know that your product crosses barriers and is loved by many cultures.

When using testimonials on your Web site, in your brochures, or on television and radio ads, seek some from customers of different nationalities and languages. Be sure to have proper translations in printed versions, and print both languages—for example, the customer's original Russian or Japanese, with English given in parentheses.

E ssential

If foreign newspapers or magazines have written about your products or services, include this information to your testimonial list with the proper translation in English. When you advertise in other countries, have your testimonials translated into that country's language as well.

One very effective method of word-of-mouth advertising is to show a real person (i.e., not a model who has been paid to be in the ad) giving his testimonial and relevant facts about himself (such as his occupation) that help make him seem real. You may have seen this approach in ads for other companies. One mattress ad uses a picture of a doctor giving a testimonial for the product and states that the doctor was not paid to endorse the product.

Ask one of your satisfied customers to introduce you to his or her friends by phone, e-mail, or in person. With a recommendation from your new prospect's friend, you've already started to build a trusting relationship.

Use as many different kinds of testimonials as possible to create word-of-mouth ads for your products and services. Word-of-mouth advertising is an essential part of creating the "yes" factor.

Chapter 15

Maintaining the Relationship

It may seem that once you sell a product or service, that is the end of the sale. But actually, once the sale is finished, the second and most important part of the sale begins. This aftersell, or second selling cycle, is where your real profit comes in. By continuing to satisfy your customer and build a relationship after the original sale has been completed, you can garner word-of-mouth praise from customers that will help you draw in business down the road.

Word-of-Mouth Advertising

There's something to be said about finding a product or service by word of mouth. If a friend, family member, or colleague is using a product or service that you like, one of the first things you might ask is "Where did you buy that?" or "Who did you use?" Word-of-mouth advertising is one of the best forms, if not the best form, of advertising you can develop—and with word-of-mouth advertising you save money on marketing, increase repeat business, and establish a strong reputation and credibility.

As you have likely discovered, it is very expensive to advertise. Expenses add up quickly regardless of which methods you choose, from television ads and fliers to Internet banners and giveaway promotional materials. Once you have spent the initial dollars and time in finding each customer, then your overall effort, time, and money is less for each sale thereafter to that same customer. If you spend approximately $1 for each successful closed sale, this dollar counts toward only one sale. However, if your customer continues to purchase items from you, then this initial dollar investment averaged across the customer's total purchases works out to less money per sale—perhaps down to seventy-five cents per sale. With their next purchase, the cost of reaching this client averaged over total purchases may drop to fifty cents. And if your loyal customer refers people to you through word-of-mouth advertising, your costs to reach customers decrease exponentially.

 Fact

Prospects become warm leads from word-of-mouth advertising. There is no better place for a sales rep to be than having prospects or customers seek you out. You have instant credibility—they know you have solved someone else's problem and they would like for you to do the same for them. This is a very warm lead from the get-go.

Once the sale is finished, this is when the second selling cycle begins. You have spent the time and money meeting with the customer and showing them who you are and what products and services you are selling that will benefit them and solve their problem. This sale now becomes the introduction of sales to come, and now you need to work on getting the subsequent sales.

Habitual Customers

Most people are creatures of habit. Once they find a business that they like, chances are they will continue to go there to make purchases. And beyond buying out of habit, if people find products and services they like, they tend to purchase them over and over.

It can be difficult for people to find good sources to get the things they want—finding the perfect combination of quality, price, and value isn't easy. So when they do find a good source, they want to keep it. That is the beauty of establishing your reputation and credibility as a great sales rep.

Target a younger audience and get them to start using your services early in their lives. If it becomes a habit you will have a customer for decades. Companies that sell credit cards and cosmetics have all used this method to get their customers while they're young, anticipating that they will continue to buy from the same company for years.

Building a Solid Reputation

Your reputation and credibility follow you wherever you go. Ask successful sales reps in the financial, manufacturing, medical, technology, and other industries—when they move to other companies, a high percentage of their existing customers follows them to their new company. Your reputation and credibility have a high value to you and your company.

This is particularly important since you may represent different companies over the span of your career. Even if you stay in the same field you are likely to move to a few different companies over the course of your career. Your best new client is your past happy client. The ideal is to build up a reputation and be known within your geographical location or industry as meeting the gold standard for honesty, professionalism, and knowledge. One of the greatest testaments to your success is knowing that people who have not even met you have heard of you. Your reputation precedes you.

Stay in Touch

Once you have closed the sale, the real selling begins. Think of the end of an original sale as the beginning of another profit center. It is very easy in sales to think that you need to keep finding new customers, keep the pipeline full, and work hard in closing these new leads. This work is the front end of the sale. And yet this is where many sales reps stop. Working the "middle" of the sale is where you'll earn your highest profit in terms of the time, effort, and money you spend to close the deal. Work with your clients to successfully make it through the two major points of the sale—the front end and the middle. The only time there is an "end" to a sale is when you have decided they are not going to be customers anymore.

Working the Middle of the Sale

Successful sales reps spend the majority of their time working the middle of a sale rather than the front end of one. The middle of a sale includes follow-up: responding promptly to questions, calls, and e-mail; getting all the information to people that they requested so that they can make a more informed decision; and checking in to find out how the product or service is solving their problem or enhancing a situation after the sale has closed.

The middle of a sale is all about maintaining the customer relationship. One of the most effective ways to maintain this relationship is with the tools you already have. These tools are the phone, e-mail, mail, your database (as described in Chapter 9), and your personality.

Reminding Them You Care

Contacting your customers on a regular basis just to say hi and see how they are doing will remind them of you and show them that you care about them and value their continued business. Sending gifts such as tickets to see a play or sporting event or a gift certificate to a restaurant adds to the goodwill they'll feel toward you.

When a customer feels that a sales rep cares about them, then the relationship grows stronger and is more easily maintained. Just because you have a customer today does not mean you will still have him or her as a customer tomorrow. Just as you nurture and care for a garden of flowers so they will bloom, you must nurture and care for your prospects and customers for sales to bloom.

E-mail is a wonderful invention for many reasons. Leave your e-mail address in your outgoing voice mail address so that clients have another way to reach you. As a tool in maintaining the relationships of your customers, e-mail is priceless. Not only can you reach your whole database in one swoop to share information about a new product or service, you can personalize each one of these e-mails as well. This saves thousands upon thousands of dollars in stamps, stationery, envelopes, and time.

Alert

E-mail addresses are as important today as phone numbers. You may return e-mails before you return calls. In addition, by sending e-mail, you avoid playing telephone tag. There is one caveat, however. Don't rely on staying in touch only via e-mail because at some point, there needs to be more personal contact—either over the phone or by meeting in person.

Staying connected by postal mail is important, but the efficiency of e-mail has reduced the need to send out as many collateral pieces by postal mail. Nonetheless, keep your database of addresses as current as possible by sending material through postal mail at least once or twice a year.

Face-to-Face Contact

There is nothing like seeing, hearing, and looking at another person when trying to maintain a relationship. When e-mail came into common use many years ago, large companies thought at first that they would save a great deal of money on travel to visit clients. They thought that maintaining a relationship via e-mail would be all that is needed. Many of the CEOs of these companies found out the hard way that clients were being lured away from them and forming new relationships with individuals who took the time to visit and maintain the relationship in person or by phone. E-mail just isn't the same. It is not necessary to maintain the relationship in person all the time, but you need to touch base with personal contact several times a year to maintain a healthy business relationship with your customers.

Continue to Sell to Your Happy Customers

Your existing clients and customers are the best people to sell more products and services to. They know you, and they know where you are located. They feel comfortable working with you because you have established a relationship with them.

Some customers may stay with you out of habit because it is easier to stay with you than to make the effort to search for another company or sales rep or investigate other products and services. These are not your primary customers, though, because these are not the customers who will refer you to others.

Some customers stay with you because they like your products and services. They are interested in hearing about new and improved items and services. Once you have successfully completed the sale, your customer is far more open to any news, new products, or new services that you may have to offer.

You've spent a great deal of money and time screening your prospect who is now a client or customer. You understand your customer's needs and wants; you have an "in" with the consumer. You now have a better idea of the needs and wants of this customer based on her demographic data, what she purchased, and (hopefully) the testimonial you received about how pleased she is with the product and the buying experience.

Your Database Is Your Inventory

Your database is not just important, it is priceless. It works for you today and in the future, no matter what field you're in. Successful sales reps keep in contact with people they have met on planes, at social functions, at business conferences, and through past clients. As a result they have built-in resources that span the globe.

Think of each of the people you capture for your database as a part of your inventory. If you can visualize each contact as a tangible piece of inventory, you may handle each contact with more care and not take it lightly. You wouldn't throw out or ignore a piece of furniture in your warehouse, if you owned a furniture business, or toss away a piece of jewelry if you ran a jewelry store. Just as furniture and jewelry are tangible pieces that have the potential to bring in money to a business, so is each person in your database a tangible and potential income-producing "item" in your inventory.

Keep your inventory—your database—clean and fresh. It's important to periodically clean it out and update it. To keep your mailing list clean, you need to send material out at least twice a year. If mail comes back with a forwarding address or is marked undeliverable, change your database entry accordingly or contact your prospect by phone or e-mail to get a more recent address. To keep your e-mail list clean, provide a place on your Web site where your customers can make changes to their e-mail address (or other contact information, as well).

 Fact

Consumers change their physical location and phone numbers more often than they change their e-mail addresses. If you lose people from your regular mail database because they have moved, drop them an e-mail. They may still have the same e-mail address and can update their other contact information for you.

Hand your business card to everyone you meet within five minutes of meeting them. And always be sure to get their card as well. You never know who might need your products or services, or when.

Take quick notes about each person you just met on the back of the card to help you remember him later. Write down important information about the person, including his hobbies or business, on the back of the business card. Describe what she looks like, where you met them, and whom else you were with. All of these things can help jog your memory later. Then, when you get to your computer to add the information to your database, include the notes you jotted down in the notes section of your customer management system. This way you'll always have it at your fingertips.

One excellent way to help manage the inventory in your database is to create groups that fit with the way you work. Groups help you to sort the people in your database into related categories that you can pull up rapidly for targeted marketing. For instance, if you do business in many locations, you might want to create groups based on geographical location of customers, making it easy to find your clients and customers in each location. This kind of sorting ability can also be very useful to your support people as well.

Ask, Listen, and Hear Feedback

All you have to do is ask. If you ask your prospects and clients what they want, what they like about a product or service, what they don't like, or what you can do to make their experience working with you better, in most cases, they will tell you.

The best market research you can do is to ask your customers what they like and dislike about the product and their experience with their purchase. You'll glean the most information from their answers if you start asking these questions at the beginning of each selling process and then continue to ask on a regular basis to get a feel for how their opinions change as they learn about your product. And it is essential to ask these questions when your prospect or customer is unhappy about any aspect of the product or service. This is damage control—finding out what people are dissatisfied with and then doing something about it prevents or sharply reduces the number of customers you lose.

When you are in the "ask and listen" mode with your prospects or customers, you are getting information about what they want, why they want it, what is important to them, and what type of service they are most interested in. You open up your mind and take the attitude that gathering information will help you solve your prospect's or customer's problem or improve a situation. To ask and listen is to retain customers, resolve errors, and prevent miscommunication.

Primary Focus on the Top 20 Percent

As discussed in earlier chapters, there is an 80-20 rule in business, called the Pareto principle, that states that 80 percent of your profits comes from 20 percent of your customers, and that 80 percent of your time is spent dealing with just 20 percent of your customers. How do you determine who the top 20 percent of your customers are? Simply calculate which customers produce 80 percent of your profits. Track this information in your database and accounting files.

Determine who your top 20 percent are and what their primary needs as a group are. Develop strategies to stay in close contact with them. This does not mean that you forget about your other customers. But it is worth developing a primary focus on the targeted populations from which your top 20 percent of customers come.

There are several excellent strategies you can use to maintain a strong relationship with your targeted group of customers. Plan an event once or twice a year for them to show your appreciation for their business. If you don't know what to do for them, ask them! You might have your executive team contact your targeted group every six weeks or so to see how they are doing. This lets them know that their business is valued by everyone at the company. Use a variety of methods to keep up contact. You can contact them one time with a phone call, the next time via e-mail, and perhaps a third time with a personal note in the mail. (Make sure that you have all their contact information in your database.)

Information you should garner for your customer database, beyond the standard contact and account information, includes the name of the spouse, names and ages of children, what your customer's hobbies are, and anything else that is important to your customer. The more you know about your top 20 percent the more genuine contacts you can make.

People love to feel special and well taken care of. What type of program can you create for your top 20 percent that gives them special access or special treatment? Establish a marketing budget for activities, collateral material, and special programs to satisfy the needs and wants of this profitable group.

Then do the same for the second tier of customers—the next 50 percent of profitable customers. Create programs that take their interests and needs in consideration as well and target them as a group.

As you start to delve into these two groups, you will find many similarities within each of the groups, but your mission is to also find the differences. Focus on the differences you find and look for ways to adjust your marketing strategies based on these differences to increase your profit.

Chapter 16

Negotiations

You negotiated with yourself the last time you made a decision about purchasing a product or service. Perhaps you bought what you needed but did not buy the top-of-the-line product you wanted. You negotiated with yourself about what was most important to you. There are several important points to consider during any negotiation. You must establish yourself as a partner, find out why your prospects and customers bought or did not buy in the past, and learn the strategies to help you succeed in every negotiation.

Positioning Yourself as a Partner

You first want to position yourself as a partner to your customer—someone who is looking out for her best interests as you help her get what she needs. Many customers continue buying from people who they feel have a vested interest in them and their purchases. If you're a partner, you will find that prospects and customers come to you even when you don't have the lowest prices or the nearest location. They believe the extra money and mileage are worth it if they've got you on their side, looking out for their best interests.

Your partnership with your customers adds value above and beyond any differences in price and location. Your word and integrity are a promise to them. With your attitude of "If you want it, I'll find it" or "I'll help you save time and make the best choice for you" or "If you're not happy with an item I'll take it back without any hassle to you" gives your customers assurance that you are on their side, a partner in their buying decisions.

How can you best become a partner with your prospects and customers? The answer lies in how you define *partner*. As a business partner to your clients, you will brainstorm and exchange ideas with them, become concerned with how to make and spend money, and set and reach goals together as one unit.

As a family partner to your clients, you'll make your customers feel safe talking to you about their feelings and what's going on in their lives. They will know you care about them personally, about their health and their feelings. There is the combination of a business and family partner, too—caring about your clients on both levels, their business affairs and their families, and interacting with them on an intellectual and emotional level as you set and reach mutual goals.

If you can live up to the best of each of these definitions, then your prospects and customers will feel strongly attached to you on several levels. Competitors will find it much more difficult to pull them away from you merely based on price. A healthy partnership is many times stronger than price alone when customers are making a decision to buy.

E ssential

Successful sales professionals often find that they and their customers become good friends. It's not the product that makes them a friend, but rather the service and the trusting relationship. Cultivating a sincere relationship that isn't just about making a sale has the side benefit of cultivating a friendship as well.

There are common points in establishing a partnership with your prospects and customers. This is one more reason to host a yearly or semiannual signature event for your prospects, clients, and friends. Events like these help cultivate a feeling of partnership.

Your customer's goals have to become your goals. The fastest way to reach a goal is to focus and create options to attain it. If you focus on your customer's goals first, then your goals as a sales rep will be met automatically in most situations. However, the reverse is rarely true. If you focus on your goals first, your customer's goals may not be met, and you may lose a customer.

Brainstorm and exchange ideas with each other. This is where you discover the core values of your prospects and customers and learn why they want and need to buy your products or services. You can also take a personal interest. Be someone who cares about your clients' business and personal lives. Everyone wants to feel special and cared for. You can interact on an intellectual and emotional level. Take the opportunity to discuss information, different generations of the product or service, how it has evolved over time. You may decide to set and reach goals together. There is more synergy, which equates to higher productivity, when two people pursue their goals together.

Finding Out Why People Bought

Whether you're speaking to a prospects or people who are already customers, it is important to learn whether they've ever bought this or a similar product or service in the past. If they have, find out what they liked and disliked about their purchase. This will help you to know how you can meet their needs and wants with this purchase, including helping you know what kind of aftercare you can provide.

If they've used a product before, their opinion and experience with it was likely in one of two categories: positive or negative. Positive responses usually come from the purchases that fulfill a core value. The product met a pressing and timely need or want; the buyer wanted an "experience"; the purchase was perceived as convenient, saved time, and saved money. It helped the customer become a better parent, student, spouse, person, or businessperson, or it benefited the family, the kids, or someone else.

A negative response can occur when the product or service didn't hold up—the money he spent didn't seem worth it once he had the product. Or perhaps the customer couldn't make a decision, so shemore or less randomly picked one of the choices available, or she felt pushed into buying the products or services.

Use the information that you learn from people's past experiences to help them get the right product or service for them this time around.

Basic Strategies to Successful Negotiation

A successful negotiation includes dialogue, arriving at mutually beneficial terms, and a discussion that produces an acceptable agreement. Successful negotiation involves understanding what the prospect or customer really wants.

Have Alternatives

Are there any other products that may do the basic job your prospect wants but are less expensive? Or that break less often? This is where product knowledge is paramount and relates directly to your sales results.

With services, you may be able to tailor an approach that meets the basic needs and wants of the prospects or customers but omits the bells and whistles that they don't want or that cost more than they want to spend. Consider creating three tiers of services, each with its own identity, benefits, and price. Generally, offering multiple levels of service helps in negotiation, because people love to have choices and to feel that they're able to select an option that truly fits their needs. This is common with products but works with services as well.

Understanding Personality and Negotiation Patterns

One kind of impasse that you may encounter in negotiating can arise from a prospect's or customer's indecisiveness. This kind of individual has trouble making decisions and may seek answers to a swarm of inconsequential questions. To halt this behavior, try asking the customer what it would take for him to move forward.

Where does the negotiation stall or slow down? Keep a record of this information in a journal. You may find that the slowdown usually occurs in the same part of the negotiation process. Once you identify where this is, you can look for ways to get around it in future negotiations. For example, look for ways to create alternatives for specific impasses or unearth facts about the product or service that better support the price.

Add Value to the Perception of Price

Aftercare is a hot button for many consumers today. Buying at large warehouse stores that sell products cheap but with little customer service has left many consumers burned by products that didn't last or are unsuited to their needs. You can lessen, if not eliminate, their insecurity by offering aftercare or a guarantee. You will find that most successful businesses have a lenient return policy, and many also have guarantees that let customers try a product or service for free for a short period. Think about how can you make it easier for your prospect or customer to try your products and services in a "safe" environment.

However, you also need to feel that you haven't compromised your core values, or your prospect's or client's! Negotiation usually stops when one side feels its integrity and core values are in jeopardy. If you can be sensitive to this and know what might trigger those feelings in the other person, you will be that much closer to moving the sale forward.

The Win-Win-Win Approach

A truly successful negotiation is one in which everyone wins at least something important to them. The old and discouraging approach to negotiation was that one person wins and therefore the other person loses; this is not a negotiation that will leave everyone feeling good about it. Positive thinking begets positive actions. Rather than focusing on what you don't have or didn't get in the negotiation, look at what you do have and the experiences and process it took to get there. If you want more positive negotiations, you need to bring more positivity to the table, and that starts with your thoughts and actions.

 Fact

One effective way to bring in more sales is to turn your positive thoughts into positive behavior by taking actionable steps. Focus on what you want, visualize yourself getting there, and positively assert affirmative statements.

A true positive partnership is one that is a win-win situation all the way around—from the manufacturer or creator to the end user. Prospects and customers feel they've won the "prize" by finding you and buying your products or services. They must feel their purchase will help them fulfill a core value and core need. You win by making a sale.

Every time a customer buys a product, the manufacturer receives a signal that the product is a hit. Every time someone buys a service, the visionary or creator behind the service earns feedback that the service fulfills a need. Every time you sell your product or service, you should feel good to know that you are truly helping your prospect or customer live life more fully.

No Need to Be Right

If you sometimes feel the need to let the other person know you're right, even if it causes a problem, stop now. Perhaps your calculations are accurate and their perceptions are wrong, and you will save someone a lot of money and time if they would only do it your way. Even if that is true, all you can do is share your experiences and hope the other person listens. If she doesn't, she will have to find the solution herself, either the easy or the hard way. You can't force someone to do something no matter how hard you try. However, you can make suggestions and give examples of how your approach helped others.

 Alert

Your ego may be guiding you if you find yourself needing to be right more times than not. How important is it to you to always be right with your prospects or customers? Focus on solving your customer's problems rather than showing how much you know. This focus will establish a trusting relationship with your customer that usually transfers into sales.

Your ego is important to keeping you motivated and active, but it can get in the way when you become the main spotlight in the selling process.

Is the customer always right? Of course not. However, there are ways to help you overcome the urge to point out that you're right when you know the customer is wrong, and they may have an effect on the selling process. Allow the customer to be wrong. It is his perception of the facts that matters most. Do not take his comments personally; try to get to the root of what he is saying.

Addressing Negative Comments

If you hear adverse comments from your customers during the middle or end of the selling process, you may be overlooking some needs and wants of theirs that are emotionally charged, and your prospects may not feel you have heard or validated them in these areas. You build a successful selling relationship if you don't hear or validate your prospect's or customer's concerns, problems, and fears.

When you experience adversity from prospects and customers at the beginning of the sales process, then you may need to open up the conversation more to establish a better relationship. Most adverse comments are a reflection of some type of uncertainty, fear, or anger. It is important to help your prospect or client get her emotions out before you think about presenting her with product or service information. You can record any reasons you come up with to account for a difficult negotiation and at what stage trouble occurred in Appendix F: Sales Rejection Analysis Sheet.

Much of negotiation deals with the psychology of selling. Most people enjoy getting good deals, no matter how much money they have. You don't have to look any further than the free samples at cosmetic counters, Costco, and Trader Joe's, or the variety of specialty advertising in the form of free T-shirts, caps, and other paraphernalia given to prospects and customers. When in the throes of negotiation, always remember to give the other person something perceived as valuable and work toward a win-win-win finale.

Chapter 17

The Telephone as Friend or Foe

The telephone has always been a key part of the salesperson's arsenal. These days, cell phone technology is so advanced that people can use their phones not only to make and receive calls, but to browse on the Internet, send text messages, download music and video, and even take pictures. Chances are the telephone is the lifeblood of your business. Even as the Internet becomes more sophisticated, people will likely depend on voice communications—whether by traditional phone, cell phones, VoIP, or new Webcams and videophones—for years to come.

Using the Telephone for Business

Many sales professionals find the phone more of a foe than friend because they are exhausted at the end of the day from the onslaught of phone calls. Now that people depend on cell phones more than landlines, nearly everyone can call and be contacted at any time of the day or night. The best way to turn your phone into a friend is for you to control it, rather than to let it control you and your schedule.

Many sales professionals believe that they need to keep their phones on at all times, no matter what they're doing. As a result, they develop negative feelings about phone use that interfere with their productivity levels. Some of these myths are:

- You need to be on call at all times of the day and night.
- Answering phone calls takes only a minute.

- A cell phone saves you time when you use it.

Believing these three telephone myths can prevent sales reps from using the phone to stimulate and maintain business. It is best to examine the truth behind these common misconceptions in order to understand how to best use the phone to your advantage as a businessperson.

 Fact

> The telephone is a helpful necessity for most sales professionals—make it your friend, not your enemy. As long as you control the time you stay on the phone, how often you take incoming calls, and when you return them, you will be averting phone exhaustion and be able to save time and energy every day.

Knowing When to Turn It Off

When you have a toothache, does your dentist take your middle-of-the-night phone call himself? If you're sick with the flu, does your doctor stop what he or she is doing and talk to you on the phone personally? Probably not. So why do sales professionals think they need to be available to customers by phones on their nights and weekends? To believe that you, as a sales rep, should take calls from your customers at any time can prove costly. Once you have trained your customers to think that you are available all the time, you will find yourself constantly bombarded with calls and "emergencies" that were never emergencies at all. These calls will rob you of energy by causing stress and anxiety. They'll steal quality time you could have spent with family or on more important work.

Do not accept every call as it comes in, and do not return calls all day long. Even though it may seem that the cost is small because it "only takes a minute" to take or make a call, this is usually not the case.

Alert

If you're in a field that deals with life-and-death situations and you are on call, you need to answer your phone whenever it rings. For all other industries, you have a choice as to when you will answer and return calls. You are not a slave to your phone, unless you choose to be.

Every time you answer the phone, you get off task from the project you were working on, and there is a higher chance of making errors when you are interrupted during a task. It is important to keep in mind that the amount of time it costs you to take a call is not only made up of the length of the actual phone conversation. You must also consider the amount of time it requires to get back on track after you have been distracted.

Setting Aside Time for Calls

The best solution to losing time making phone calls throughout the day is to cluster calls in specific time slots. Plan a time, preferably the same time each day, to make and return calls. Keep your schedule open from 11:00 A.M. to noon for incoming calls while you do work that does not require your total concentration. Use this time to return several calls together, or e-mail follow-up responses to phone messages. Keep your schedule open again for incoming calls between 4:00 P.M. and 5:00 P.M. and return more calls during this time. If you have five or ten minutes free before a meeting, you can use this time to make or return calls and e-mails as well.

With this method, you don't have to stop to think about whether to let a call to go to your voice mail, because you have two "formal" times to make and return calls every day. You don't have to worry that you won't have time to get back to your prospects or customers in a timely fashion, because you have set up a system to get it done.

Establishing a Schedule

Be sure to let your customers know in your outgoing message when you plan to return calls to give them assurance that you will get back to them. Cluster calls to two or three times daily. When you return several calls one after another, you're on a roll and you create time in your day for follow-up, research, or aftercare—the primary reasons you make and return calls to begin with. Keep a list for a few days to identify what type of incoming and outgoing calls you make most. Are they mainly to give or receive information, to do follow-up, to touch base, or something else?

The Good and Bad of Phone Use

If you stay in control, cell phones and landlines will save you time. But if you accept every incoming call as it arrives, during meals, drives, and meetings, they won't. And worse, they'll actually interfere with your customer service, project concentration, and quality time—affecting not only you but also your family, friends, and other customers.

You also lose quality time with family and friends when you allow phone calls to interrupt your time. Every time you accept a call or even check to see who is calling, you are disrupting what you were focusing on, whether it is work, relaxing, sleep, or planning. It is up to you to establish boundaries as to when and where you will accept calls. The only rule of thumb is to always return calls within twenty-four hours.

Cell phones don't save you time if you get in a fender-bender because you were concentrating on your phone conversation rather than on the road. They don't save you time if you lose the interest of a prospect or customer because you've accepted a call in the middle of a meeting. And you lose inspiration or creative thought mid-conversation in a meeting because you're distracted by the vibration of the phone and checking to see who called.

The Best Time to Make Calls

It helps to think of phone calls as meetings. In an hour-long meeting, most of the important information and events occur near the end. The same thing happens with the telephone. If you know beforehand that you can spend no more than five minutes on the phone, you get to the meat of the conversation or business at hand faster without spending (or wasting) time just chitchatting. Clients often say that they are spending "only a few minutes" on the phone, but those few minutes usually last far longer than they anticipate or even realize. Then the time crunch of the day starts, as you lack the extra ten or thirty minutes you need to complete a task, drive in extra traffic, or handle myriad other things. Without getting stressed out, make every minute count.

The Value of Each Moment

Think about the Olympic gold medal winner who wins by a fraction of a second, the car accident you avoided by seconds, the missed extra second when the time for a test is up, the extra minutes you sit in traffic, or the few extra minutes it takes to take your dinner from raw to a delicious dish. Every moment of your day can be valuable.

Think also in terms of five-minute intervals. If you find you have five or ten minutes suddenly free in the day, such as when you're waiting for a meeting to start or when one ends early, this is a good time to make those calls that you know won't take much time. You can make the most of your day by taking care of as many of these short business calls at times when you would normally be unoccupied but don't have enough time for lengthy phone conversations. They're quick, easy, and specific—the best of all worlds.

Essential

Decide in advance how much time you need to have an effective phone conversation with prospects, clients, and vendors. Keep your calls to five minutes or less. Use a kitchen timer to get in the habit of knowing how long you are on the phone.

The best time to make calls is during a low-energy period of the day. It is important to know your energy patterns. Do you have the most energy in the early mornings, late mornings, early or late afternoons, or evenings? Once you have identified your energy patterns, you can work to maximize your time. If you have high energy in the mornings, don't waste that energy making phone calls. You will be more productive doing work that requires thinking, creativity, and brain power so that you are at your peak in these areas. When you come up for air after an hour or two, then you'll likely still have high energy levels, but you may need a break. This may be a perfect time to make your most important calls: marketing calls, calls to prospects and customers with a pending purchase, any call that requires listening closely to conversations.

Keep the calls that require troubleshooting to your calling period before lunch. Again, your energy will still be up, but you'll have a level of confidence that comes from having taken care of work and gotten things done. You'll be more available emotionally to creatively go through the troubleshooting process.

Stress is one of the biggest energy and time drainers that exists. You want to be smart about handling potentially stressful situations. You want to take care of them, but you don't want to get caught up in them. When you feel yourself getting upset or stressed, take sixty seconds to take in several deep breaths and think positive thoughts. It's a great way to quickly cool down and continue working.

Become Familiar with Others' Time Patterns

Most people have daily patterns, and they may make calls consistently at a certain time. This is often the best time to catch them when you're returning or making phone calls. To recognize this pattern, it is important to know when the person phones you. If you regularly receive calls from clients, vendors, or others at certain times a day, it is a good idea to make a note of the times that work well for them.

Document the time of day each client calls and in short order you will usually find a pattern. If a client calls you at 8:30 A.M. one day, for instance, you may have good luck in getting her to pick up the phone around that same time the next day. However, don't become dependent on making calls all day long just to work around others' schedules. This is a good approach to take mainly when you are having trouble making contact with someone.

Fact

Just before lunch is a good time to make and return calls. Many people are in their offices around 11:30 A.M. as they try to finish a task before lunchtime. People also often check messages on their way to lunch and you may get a callback sooner, and chances are the call will be shorter as the clock ticks toward lunchtime.

As a general rule, the best times to return calls are before lunch, around 11:15 A.M., and before leaving the office for the day, around 4:15 P.M. This is also a good time to connect with hard-to-reach people who have left voice mail messages for you, especially if they lack e-mail access or prefer to do most of their transactions by phone.

Try not to make troubleshooting calls first thing in the morning, as you may feel stressed the rest of the day if the calls do not go as planned. You will eventually have to "bite the bullet" and deal with problems or cranky or unhappy customers, but you don't need to do this first thing when you get to work. Start your day productively, then make these more difficult calls an hour or two after you've started working.

Before the end of the workday is another good time to reach people, since many people are in their offices just prior to going home for the evening. People who work at home tend to stay at their desks later than their office counterparts do. This may happen because the boundary between work and home can become a bit blurred, and work can pour over into home life because the tasks, computer, and files are right there.

Another way to make contact with the person you're trying to reach has to do with what to say when you leave a message on his voice mail. Be specific about when you will be available to talk in the next couple of days. This helps you to prevent playing telephone tag. You can also suggest that he drop you an e-mail stating specifically what he needs.

Points to Make in Your Voice Mail

Can you imagine how chaotic and time-consuming life would be without a way to leave messages by phone? Leaving messages on voice mail is an ideal way to get across exactly what you want to the other person, even when they aren't available to take your call. Many times, people prefer to leave a voice mail message rather than to leave a message with an assistant or receptionist. Voice mail gives the recipient specific information and there is less potential for miscommunication.

When you leave a voice mail message for someone else, it is important to be clear and specific. There are several ways to do this effectively. Leave all the necessary information including the time and date you called. If you need to ask a question, go ahead and do it, and specifically request that the person leave the answer on your voice mail or e-mail if they don't reach you in person. Ask too whether he prefers that you use voice mail or e-mail. Some information is confidential and you want to be sensitive to this.

Always leave your e-mail address and phone number even if you know the person you are contacting already has this information. This saves them time because they don't have to look up your information, and you'll get your call or e-mail returned sooner. Even though finding the number may take only a minute, those minutes add up and often that's just enough reason for someone to say, "I'll do it later." Looking up the number or e-mail address takes them off task, and they may easily get distracted by another project and not return your call quickly, if at all.

If you are trying to set up a meeting, leave a message that includes two or three dates and times that work for you. When your prospect returns the call or e-mail, she can simply choose the date and time that works for her. This will make your time flow better. And if she responds by e-mail, you don't lose time chatting, either.

Avoiding Phone Tag

Telephone tag is a huge waste of time and a drain on energy, and it can cause various levels of stress. It drains your energy because you may tend to get irritated when you have trouble reaching someone, especially when you can't complete a task until you do. It may also cause anxiety if you are approaching a deadline and having trouble contacting the person you need for further essential information or confirmations.

The best ways to cut out games of telephone tag are to include your e-mail address in your voice mail message and ask the person to send e-mail, specify on your voice mail message the best times to contact you, and leave specific messages about what you want or specific answers to questions you've received by phone or e-mail.

E ssential

If you're on vacation, do not check your work-related phone messages and e-mail. If you do, you'll be absent from work physically but not emotionally. Give yourself a break on vacation, and let your mind clear. If you don't, you may return to work just as frazzled as when you left.

If you will be out of the office for longer than two days, mention this fact on your voice mail message so people don't think that you are just not returning their calls. You may also share with them that you will be checking your phone messages and e-mail (if you will be) and the name of an alternate person to contact (with extension number) if you are not planning to check in or in case they need to speak with someone urgently.

When to Use E-Mail

There just isn't enough time in most business days to make and return all the calls you need to, so you'll probably be tempted to bring these calls home and infringe upon your family or regenerative time. Instead, intertwine e-mail with calls. How do you know whom to e-mail, and when? There are a couple of ways you can do this.

If you have talked with the client or prospect several times recently, it may not be necessary to have another phone conversation.

E-mailing the information you want to give them gets the job done without wasting time. If you feel you need to talk, of course, then you should. But using e-mail for correspondence that doesn't require a phone conversation can help ease the calling burden and save you a great deal of time. Not only that, but the other person will be happy you got back to him within the day. The rule of thumb is that you respond to the other person within twenty-four hours, unless you're dealing with a time-sensitive transaction that must be handled more quickly.

Using Your Voice Mail to Direct Calls

Used to its fullest, voice mail acts as your virtual assistant. It lets you capture the entire message, including voice inflection, which is something you don't get with e-mail. If you'll be out of town or otherwise unavailable, ask a colleague to cover for you while you're out of touch. (And then do the same for that person when she needs it.) Develop a team of other professionals whom you trust and share strengths with. Leave information in your outgoing voice mail message about how callers can contact these other team members who are covering for you. It is important, so if you do not have such an arrangement, you may want to think about developing one. You never know when you'll need your team members. And your customers will appreciate not having to wait when they can't reach you.

 Fact

Every sales rep functions best with a team. Your team members may include people you trust to get back to clients by phone or e-mail, people who will pick up items for you when you're out of town, and someone who can do your banking for you in a pinch or pick up your children in case of emergency.

A major pitfall of being reliant on technology like voice mail and e-mail lies in the occasional breakdown of such systems. To minimize misunderstandings, remember that when you send an e-mail and have not received a response by e-mail or phone within a day, call to make sure the e-mail arrived. When you leave a phone message and don't hear back by phone or e-mail, send an e-mail message and call again. Just like the phone, the computer is only as good as the person who controls and manages it. Don't let miscommunication occur just because of a technology glitch!

Chapter 18

Organization as a Success Tool

One of the keys to a successful sales career is keeping your time and materials in check. Good organization is the only way to keep track of what you're doing, where you are, and where you want to go. Everything needs a space or a home. From e-mail subscriptions to magazine articles, you need the ability to find everything at a moment's notice. Organization has become more and more difficult as the sheer amount of information available multiplies. But that just means it's more valuable to be organized now than ever before.

Get Focused

The ability to focus and organize is one of the primary tools to achieving success in your sales career. The first step toward productivity is organization. There are many important areas to consider when developing organizational points and outlines, flow charts, or file systems for easy retrieval. Your effort to do all you can to stay organized will be repaid many times over.

Think of all the tools you will need to be organized: a customer management system for organizing your prospects and customers, a daily planner or Palm Pilot for organizing your calendar, and a filing system (a mobile one, if you do a lot of traveling) for organizing your files. Organize files for prospects and clients (keep files of active and inactive customers separate), product information, services, and personal files that you may need instant access to.

Every piece of paper needs a storage home. There should be a designated spot for everything, so you can put it away without having to think about where it goes. Divide your filing system into general categories with subtopics within each general topic file. Your filing system works just like an organized outline. For instance, you may have a general file called "money" that includes subcategories related to finances such as travel expenses, client expenses, marketing and PR expenses, car mileage and expenses, and commissions by month. Under the general category of marketing and PR, you would include subcategories for the individual marketing avenues you use (such as newspaper advertising or Internet/Web site advertising) and companies that you hire to handle PR. The more specific each subcategory, the more organized you will feel.

Keep Records of Goals, Calls, and Income

Develop a system to keep good track of essential information. The level of detail you choose to go into is up to you, but there are some basic rules you can follow to get started. Creating a useful system of organization lies in asking yourself the right questions so that you establish a system that makes it possible to retrieve important information and view useful data easily.

Alert

Don't leave anything to memory—write it down. It's the little things that make the difference between ordinary and extraordinary. You want to go after the extraordinary in customer care and follow-up. The busier you get, the harder it is to remember things that you have not written down.

A set of goals is like a roadmap of where you want to go. Writing down the goals gives you more impetus and energy to complete them. Looking at your goals daily increases motivation and focus. And the energy and motivation that you get from focusing on your goals will help propel them into being. By looking at them often, you make them of utmost importance in your mind. Because goals are such an important aspect of succeeding in your business and in your life, it is wise to develop a system that allows you to locate, modify, or change them at a moment's notice. You could keep your goals in a journal, a workbook, or a computer file. Some types of goals that you may make include the number of calls you make daily, the number of prospects you convert to customers, and the top priorities to accomplish each day. You might also keep a list of the top five values that you want to maintain in your business—that's another type of goal.

A list of your daily goals will also help you concentrate on getting tasks done. Write them down at the same time you make your to-do list or at the top of the calendar for each day. Review them several times during the day to help keep yourself on track. It is amazing how easy it is to get off task in your busy sales life.

Contact Information

Contacts are the lifeblood of your business. Contacts can come by telephone or e-mail or even in person, but the bottom line is that you want to capture all the people who contact you. To make your life a little easier, always ask for e-mail addresses, just as you would ask for the phone number or mailing address. The primary reason to capture these e-mail addresses is that you will be able to stay in communication with your prospects and customers easily and consistently with less effort than a phone call takes. As you develop your system and get to know your clients, you will be able to decide which people to e-mail information to and which ones to call to get the best results.

Some of the factors to consider in this organizational process are the needs of your callers. Do they want a simple piece of information or do they need to discuss an issue with you in detail? Divide the calls to be returned into two piles: those asking a follow-up question and those you have to phone or meet in person.

Following Up

Remember the e-mail-to-phone-call ratio. It's important to keep connected with your customers by phone, but a 5:1 ratio works well: E-mail five times for every phone call you make to that customer. The time-saving virtues of e-mail are excellent when you are playing the sometimes endless game of phone tag.

 Fact

E-mail addresses are just as important as phone numbers today. It is easier, more convenient and cost-effective to get and stay in contact with prospects and clients via e-mail. E-mail prevents games of telephone tag, can be done at any time, and is checked more often than voice messages in the business world.

You will find in Appendix C a Customer Call Follow-Up Sheet. This is a very easy system to use that works well for keeping track of the contact you have with each prospect or customer. Fill out the call sheet after each phone call, and put the information into your database as soon as possible afterward. If you're at your computer at the time of the call, you can skip the paper version of the form and enter the data directly into your database.

Money passes quickly through your hands or bank accounts. Knowing where your money comes from and where it is going will help you control it effectively. Develop an organized system that allows you to identify how much money you make, what percentage of your total income comes from each client, and the average purchase per person. You will also find it useful to know the demographics and psychographics (see Chapter 6) of the top 20 percent of your most profitable clients. Also identify and manage the amount of money you save each month. It is not so much how much you *make* but how much you *keep*.

Keep Records of Prospects and Client Contacts

You understand by now the importance of capturing information about your prospects and customers in a database. You can purchase database packages known as customer relationship management (CRM) programs. You want to track each contact you make with a prospect or customer in your CRM program so you know exactly what you said to them when and what you sold to them.

CRM databases are extremely useful, popular, and customer-friendly. Online retail Web sites already use this software to keep track of every purchase a customer makes and to cross-sell to them, suggesting other items they may want to buy based on what they've purchased (or even what they've searched for) in the past.

By keeping detailed information on your prospects and clients, you too can offer them additional products and services they may want based on the interest they've expressed in the past. When you set up your CRM database, you can define a category for specific products or services, so that when a customer purchases one, this category gets checked off. You can then query your database, ask for all customers who bought an item in this particular category, and e-mail them to let them know about another product in that category that they may be interested in.

Keep a Clear Desk for a Clear Mind

Most sales professionals have so many papers and sticky notes lying around that their workstations look like a tornado has struck them. Searching for items right in front of you wastes precious time and depletes your energy, diminishing your effectiveness. It is important that your work area is neat and clear when you enter it in the morning. Otherwise, you will lose time and mental energy the moment you get to your desk. Most sales professionals feel highly motivated and energized in the mornings if their desks are clear.

E ssential

Instead of keeping office supplies like your stapler, sticky notes, paperclips, and notepaper on top of your desk, use a drawer to hold all of these items. When you are working in your office, you will be able to focus on high priority work instead of being overwhelmed by clutter. A messy desk will stop you cold in your productivity tracks.

At the end of the day, put your papers into stacks with your sticky notes on top that identify what's in each stack. Place the stacks in a drawer or on a table or bookshelf—anywhere but your desk. If you are pressed for space, place the stacks under your desk—as long as you can't see them at first glance into your work area. You will feel a difference in the morning when your desk is clear and neat.

Take just five minutes a few times a day to file papers. You will be amazed at how much filing you can do in just five minutes! There are always papers that you intend to get back to immediately, but then don't. To help wean yourself from this habit, keep a folder in a drawer or away from the desk, in which you simply file these pages. At some point, you will realize that you can toss most of the papers, and you only need to deal with very few of them. If possible, keep your fax machine, printer, and computer someplace other than your desk. Keep your desk as clear as possible to encourage focused work.

Organizing Paper Files

Have you ever felt buried in paper? Do you sometimes feel like just a few days after you take the time to file papers, your desk or office look like a train wreck again? Here are a few ways to conquer paper.

 Fact

Organizational companies suggest making a small dot at the top of every piece of paper each time you handle it, even if you are just moving it from one pile to another. They have discovered that a piece of paper with ten dots or more is probably no longer necessary to keep around.

Start by writing down the topics of the papers strewn around your desk and office. You will find that several similar categories keep coming up. This will help you to identify what categories you should create in your file system for these papers. File the papers in these new file folders with the most recent papers on top. This approach improves your organization further and saves time and energy when you're looking up something.

Go through this process until there is a file for every piece of paper that passes through your hands. And don't forget about the wastebasket. When in doubt about whether you need a particular piece of paper, place it in a miscellaneous folder. If after a month you still don't know what to do with it, it may be okay to toss it.

The more detailed your file categories are, the easier and faster it will be for you to retrieve important papers. As you develop your organizational filing chart, make copies of this list and place them at the front of each drawer in your filing cabinet. The most effective way to file for sales reps is to either color code or alphabetize. For example, your money files could be green and your client files could be yellow. Or you can alphabetize general categories, like applications and contracts.

Organizing E-Files

Sometimes it takes a technological glitch that takes down your e-mail system to make you realize how much you depend on e-mail. You may have enormous amounts of e-mail that represent personal communication, newsletters, product information, or updates about company initiatives. Forward any e-mails that can be handled by an assistant or by someone else in your office and answer only those e-mails that you must personally answer. Create a filter to automatically catch spam as it comes in, so it goes straight to your junk e-mail box and you don't even have to see it. Once a week you may want to scan the junk folder, just to make sure the spam filter didn't mistakenly catch any important e-mails. Add legitimate e-mail addresses in your address book so that the important e-mails arrive in your inbox without being rejected as spam.

Automatic Response

Use the auto response feature of your e-mail software to send out an immediate response to everyone who e-mails you. This can be customized depending on your needs of the day. It may say, "I will be returning e-mails today between 11 and 12 and between 4 and 5." If you are on vacation or unable to respond for several days, you might set up an auto-response that says, "I am out of the office and will be returning e-mails on April 24."

Timing Your Responses

To keep your focus from being derailed, do not check your e-mail first thing in the morning when you get ready to start your work. Do not check last thing at night before going to bed, either, since chances are you can't do anything about them until the workday starts, except worry. Pick a time, twice a day, to check e-mails and respond to those that need to be answered. Categorize the rest in specific folders to read at a later time.

The Anatomy of Your Calendar

Being more efficient is not just about the organization of your files. You must develop a structure to your day and organize your calendar as well. To get the most out of your day, you need to define your priorities daily as they relate to your goals. To reach your goals, you will need to create an effective structure to your day and arrange your calendar so you know what needs to be done with just a glance at it. Having daily goals will help keep you focused and on task. Write down your daily goals and prioritize your day's activities. This will structure your day and help you stay on task. Choose two important tasks at a time and focus on those two until they are completed. Then go on to the next two highest priority items. This will keep you focused and on target to reach your daily goals

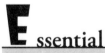

Block out time daily for completing tasks, for appointments, and for making and returning calls and e-mails. This will keep your tasks from taking up your entire day and it will also help streamline your customer and client appointments by clustering them together instead of leaving your schedule open-ended.

Structuring the Day

Structure your day so you know what top priority tasks you will be doing in the morning and which ones you will do in the afternoon. Structuring your day into morning activities and afternoon activities gives you one more level of organization to follow and keep you on track. One of the most important things you can do when structuring your day is to develop systems that keep you in check.

Organizing the Calendar

Take each calendar day and divide it into thirds. The top third focuses on morning activities and meetings, the middle third lasts from about noon until about 4:00 P.M., and the final third includes activities and meetings you schedule between 4:00 P.M. and evening. Just by a glance at your daily calendar, you can see its structure. Now take this structure one step further and organize your time according to the projects, activities, or work you will be doing. Here is a sample of a structured and organized day:

Tuesday

Goal(s):

Complete presentation

Make contact with pending prospects and clients

Priorities:

Focus on presentation

Make e-mail contact with tier 1 and tier 2 prospects and clients

Oversee one marketing strategy and measure its success rate

Daily Schedule

6:00 A.M.	Exercise
6:45 A.M.	Meditate, think about the day, read uplifting material
7:15 A.M.	Shower and prepare for work
7:45 A.M.	Eat a quick, healthy breakfast
8:00 A.M.	Take the kids to school or go directly to work
8:30 A.M.	Be at your desk ready to start your workday

8:45 A.M.	Work on tasks that require high concentration
10:30 A.M.	Return calls to tier 1 prospects and clients
11:00 A.M.	Return calls, e-mails to tier 2 and tier 3 prospects and clients
Noon	Eat lunch (definitely leave your desk)
1:15 P.M.	File papers for 10–15 minutes
1:30 P.M.	Meet with prospects, clients
4:40 P.M.	Return essential calls and e-mails to tier 1 clients
5:15 P.M.	Stack papers, files, and anything else piled on your desk so it is clear and clean
5:30-5:45 P.M.	Walk out the door
7:00 P.M.	Read, play piano, enjoy a hobby, work with children on homework
9:30 P.M.	Start your bedtime ritual of slowing down physically and emotionally

Keep your evenings clear for you to regenerate for a few hours before going to bed and starting your workday all over again. Try to keep meetings to an occasional one or two per week, preferably during the day rather than after work.

 **Question**

How can I relax at bedtime? I am usually so wound up.
Before bed, sip chamomile tea, listen to music, or do anything else that relaxes you. Do not watch or listen to the news first thing in the morning or last thing at night. You will be more productive during the day if you take time to recover each evening.

You may want to schedule two days a week primarily for working on marketing strategies: PR, customer service, follow-up, database management, meeting with centers of influence, planning, writing content for your Web site, writing content for your podcast or blog, or interviewing successful people in your field. Remember, if you do not take the lead in organizing your day, others will!

Chapter 19

Letting Others Know What You Sell

It may seem strange to think that others may not know what you are selling, when you have spent so much time, money, and energy in getting your message across. Other people often don't understand how your business works and how you make money. They may have a basic idea of what you can offer but are not clear on the full extent of your product or service line. And as a result, you are missing out on a great deal of business.

Why It's a Mystery

Because, like most sales reps, you probably don't cultivate your friends and families the way you cultivate prospects, clients, and customers, many of your family members and friends are likely not totally aware of what you do. Even your clients may not know the full extent of the products or services you have to offer. This concept is referred to as the "marketing hole." Many sales reps get increasingly frustrated because they feel that all the effort they put into their business should be giving them more bang for their time, energy, and investment, when they are overlooking a key area for expanding their business.

Missed Referrals

If your friends, family, and customers don't know what you offer, you are losing out on potential business opportunities. You are missing word-of-mouth advertising from those closest to you. You are not getting the referrals from family and friends that you could be getting, because they are not talking about the benefits of your products to the people they know. They may have a vague idea of what you do but they may not totally understand your business. To help them understand better what you have to offer, share stories about work and the results you have gotten. Share what your satisfied customers say about using you to solve their problems or enhance situations. You will be surprised at the responses you get.

Your family and friends may even be buying from your competitor because they don't know that you can help them. They may have only a vague idea of what you do. Frequently share case stories with them so that they get a good idea of the scope of what you do. Offer to help them in the same manner that you would offer any other prospect. Ask them for their business and for referrals.

Passing on the Word

If you have wowed your family and friends, they will share this information with passion when introducing you to new people. Right off the bat, the person you're introduced to will want to know more about what you do, and by chatting you may find that you can help them as well.

By giving everyone a very clear picture of what you do and what you provide, you can capitalize on opportunities to cross-sell other products and services to your existing customers who know and like you. If the people closest to you don't know exactly how you can solve their problems with your products or services, you are missing opportunities to sell to them.

Using Your Business Card Effectively

Your business card is one of the strongest statements in your marketing arsenal. Be sure that your family and friends have a stack of cards to give out to prospective customers for you. Ask them to write their names on the back of the card so that you will know where the referral came from. This will help you identify what channels are working best for you. If they can also get a business card of the person they gave your card to, all the better.

You need to pass your business card out wherever you can. Make a pledge to pass out a minimum of 1,000 business cards a year. That's fewer than three cards a day. By making this commitment, you will become very focused on using your business card as a marketing tool. If possible, redo your business card every year, to make it a little more specific and keep the design fresh. You may want to use the back side of your card to highlight three major benefits you can provide customers or other helpful information to spark their interest. Especially if your products or services are at the high end in terms of price, you may want to use raised lettering on your business card to take advantage of the statement of refinement, class, and professionalism that it conveys.

 Question

Should my business card reflect my personality or my customer's personality?
Your business cards should reflect your personality, as it is your first line of your unique branding. However, it also needs to fit your customer's and prospect's expectations of what you do.

A good business card will reflect you, your personality, and your specialty. An interior designer will have a different style of business card than a plastic surgeon. For example, if you are selling accounting services, a conservative look instills confidence in your prospect. If you are selling a creative service, such as interior design, you'll want something more fashionable. If your company promotes environmentalism, be sure to use recycled paper and investigate printing with soy ink. Your business card may be light, fun, and upbeat, or it may be simple and professional. You may include your picture, or you may have a card that is text only. Be sure that your card conveys the right message about you and your business.

Your Internet Presence

If you do not have a Web site, you should develop one. Hire a Web consultant, a graphic artist, and anyone else who can lead you in the right direction and make sure your Web site does what you need it to do. Some Web sites exist mainly to convey information about what you do and establish your credibility as a sales rep. These Web sites take the place of costly brochures for many sales reps. There are also Web sites whose prime function is to sell product. So it behooves you to decide first what type of a Web site you want and what its main purpose is. You may feel that the initial cost of starting up a site seems high, but having the right resources from the start will help you develop a strong foundation for your branding and your products and services. The cost is worth it.

Partnering on the Web

It is also helpful to partner with other Web sites and have your information on their sites as well. Partnering is a savvy marketing tool in your selling arsenal. It is imperative that you choose very carefully the Web sites you partner with, because your credibility is on the line. You want to associate with Web sites that are consistent with your values, career goals, and the image you want to present to customers. Carefully chosen partnerships make the strongest impact.

Online Newsletter Advertising

Pay attention to businesses that help you easily generate an online newsletter. They will provide the content—information and articles related to your field—and place your picture and logo at the top, and wham—you have a newsletter to send out. What if you offered to write a column or article for Web sites that target the same customer market that you're trying to reach? It helps get your name out there and brings traffic to your Web site, because each article you write will include your byline and Web site address. In your byline you can also give out information about how customers can find your podcast (if you have one). This is another reason why it is important for you to know who your customer is now and exactly what markets you would like to further target. You can easily reach new people, and you make it easy for potential customers and clients to contact you and start building a relationship. And make sure you capture each contact in your database.

The Importance of Exposure

Getting exposure is all about getting your name in front of as many people as possible, including on the Web. The more people see your name, see your picture, and read about what you can provide for them, the better chance you have of closing the sale. If people tell you they have heard of you or seen you "somewhere," you know that you are getting your name out there.

People do business with others who are familiar to them, even if they've never met them before. This is the strength in "viral" marketing, whether it is offline or online. You become more well-known each time other colleagues, sales reps, vendors, and customers spread the word about you through word-of-mouth advertising or through testimonials of your services and products, each time you give an interview for a column in an e-zine or newspaper, each letter you send, and each advertising piece that people see.

More and more sales reps are not only selling their products and services on their Web sites, but are signing up as affiliates with others to help each other cross-promote related products and services. This can be a great way to get your name in front of new potential customers who might not have heard about you yet.

Developing a Slogan Statement

Come up with a smart one- or two-sentence slogan statement that summarizes your work and includes a specific benefit or two for it. Use it anytime you introduce yourself to someone new. Make this phrase interesting and appealing so that prospects will ask for more information. This "slogan statement" is a way to get a dialogue started.

Identify Major Benefits

When sharing with another person what you do, make sure that the benefits you mention are things that will be important to that person. For example, if you're talking to a twentysomething, you may mention a different benefit than you would to a fortysomething. Let your prospect or customer know that you have helped others similar to him or her by sharing successful outcomes. This approach further educates your prospect about what you do.

Always Have Materials with You

You never know when you will meet your next customer, so you should always be prepared with some marketing materials or free samples. You may not make a sale immediately, but you will make an impact. When you make an impact on someone he or she is more likely to tell others about you, and a sale is sure to be forthcoming somewhere down the line. Each product you give away costs you money. But think of this as one of the best marketing strategies for your business. If you are selling a line of products, consider what you can give potential customers now from that line. Or you might even give them a choice of a few items you believe they would appreciate and ask them which one they would like to see or try.

Keep a list of what you give away free, to whom, the date you gave it, and an e-mail address and phone number of the person you gave it to. Leave room for comments and notes on your follow-up. At the very minimum you can ask for a testimonial for the product or service.

Giving things away may seem easier to do when you have product on hand than when you're selling an intangible service. But even with services, there are still ways to spread the word with giveaways. An idea that has worked very well for many sales reps is to identify on your calendar, approximately three months out, what different service programs you will offer. Then create a flier advertising your upcoming events or services. You may be giving a seminar in another city or offering teleseminars from the comfort of your own office. Create a flier that contains the time, price, and benefits of what you are offering. Keep these fliers with you and give them out to most of the people you come in contact with. Send out the flier to the people in your database via e-mail. This approach serves two major functions: It encourages you to plan and schedule in new programs, and it keeps you focused on ways to bring in new clients and let them know more about what you do.

Sharing Sales Goals with Others

There is something motivating about making a verbal commitment to others, and sharing your goals with another person is just that. Perhaps there is an implicit need to follow up so that you don't look like a fool or lose your integrity. You now have another person whom you must be accountable to. This is referred to as the accountability principle.

To hold yourself accountable, share your sales goals with others. Once you have officially verbalized your goals, sales projections, or new marketing strategies out loud to others, you have an extra little bit of motivation to work toward and meet these goals.

For years professionals have gotten together to share their goals with others of like mind and in similar industries. You may want to start a "goals group." To make your goals group an effective time and motivational tool, you must include only people who are genuinely enthusiastic about its success. You need to surround yourself with others like yourself.

Alert

In a goal group, confidentiality is essential, since each person is sharing a bit of his or her own goals. Outside of the gathering, no one should discuss anything that transpired, except to the person it affects directly. This is a safe group in which you should feel comfortable asking for an introduction to someone for business purposes.

It is important that the group maintain a positive attitude. Sharing goals within your goal group is not the time to hear all the downsides of new ideas. Instead, everyone should perceive all ideas as reachable. There must be genuine support; there is no room for competition or put-downs. This should be a group that you can always count on to raise your spirits and give you hope when you need it to stay motivated to reach your goals.

The participants of your goals group can be from different fields or from the same industry you're in. The most important point is that each person contributes by sharing his or her goals and helps to keep others motivated and accountable to the goals they've created for themselves.

Chapter 20

Closing the Sale

How do you close the sale? Many sales professionals find this part of the job confusing and frightening. The confusion usually occurs because many sales training classes teach several types of closes. The question becomes which type of close to use when and with whom. Fear arises because of all the focus and pressure on closing the sale. Effective sales training and coaching shows how successful closes can be easy transitions—if you use the relationship principles of the sales cycle.

The Sales Cycle

In most sales training seminars and individual coaching sessions, the ending attracts far too much attention and detracts from the rest of the selling cycle. As a result, many sales professionals get nervous. They ask themselves: How am I going to conclude this sale? Which technique do I need? There really is no close to a sale, but rather an agreement to do business at a specified time. Your responsibility as a sales professional is to continue the relationship. Interestingly, when you ask successful sales reps how they close a sale, most will tell you that sales "close themselves."

Most sales go through several phases before the customer signs on the proverbial dotted line. There are five phases to each cycle:

1. Introductory
2. Values and needs information

3. Information reflection
4. Signing
5. Aftercare

Your sales may take an average of three weeks to close, or they may take a few days or a few months. No matter how long or short your average sales cycle is, get to know the customer and let him get to know you. Show the prospect your materials and give him time to digest it all. Call back to get feedback on what he wants to do next and to answer any questions or concerns. This part of the sales cycle, the "thinking" part, often takes the longest amount of time. And once you have helped a prospect see the value and the upside of the deal, he will usually say yes, and the deal closes itself.

 **Alert**

A sale will often "close itself" if you have worked through the sales cycle. Therefore it is important for you to know the length of the typical selling cycle in your industry, where the potential weak links lie, and what to do at each stage if you see a problem coming.

The sales cycle never actually ends, because aftercare follows a sale. Aftercare will eventually turn into another cycle of selling, and the whole process will repeat itself. The second time around, the process is usually shorter and smoother; repeat customers already know what to expect of you.

There are many opportunities for weak links to occur in the selling process, and the common weak spots vary from one industry to another. However, there are some weak links that cross industry lines. One is the inability of the salesperson to reach the decision-maker. It may be due to her busy schedule, or her calls may be screened by an assistant. Another weak link that can affect sales reps in any industry is not finding a way to connect with the prospect. Finding that connection is imperative. It may be a similar interest, such as sports, or it may be a mutual acquaintance. Finally, some prospects may find your services too risky or they may not think your product fulfills a need. This often occurs when you do not adequately describe the full potential and benefits your product can offer them.

Introductory Phase

The first phase of the sales cycle is the introductory phase. First, you make introductions, exchanging first names and pleasantries with your prospect. Always thank your prospects for giving you their time and for meeting with you. After all, they could meet with a number of competitors instead of you. You may strike up a conversation about a hobby you both enjoy, such as fishing, skiing, or cooking. It is amazing how much information you can discover about a person in this phase. If you listen closely, you'll probably learn their marital and parental status, careers, a few of their quirks, some of their needs and values regarding your products or services, and much more.

Getting to know someone is of utmost importance in the selling process, and it is also what makes the selling process fun. If you cut short this part of the sequence, not only will you risk losing the sale, but you'll compromise the fulfillment you find in your career.

For the introductory phase, your interaction with your prospect may start something like this:

You: "Good morning, Mr. Jacobs. Thank you for taking the time to meet with me today. I know there are a number of other people you could have seen."

Prospect: "Well, I heard about you from Michael, and he suggested I speak with you about my business."

Create the relationship with your prospect just the same as you would with someone outside the selling process. Your prospects are people with the same needs, wants, and values as your friends. Be attentive, allow them to speak more than you, and relate to what they are saying in a conversational manner. Try to connect on a personal level at this stage. You may want to speak a bit about your respect for the person who introduced you or start a small conversation about how you both know the same person. This makes a personal connection and makes the next phases easier, because the prospect feels as if he is talking with a friend.

Values and Needs Information Phase

The next phase of the selling cycle is the values and needs information phase. After your introductory conversation, ask specific questions that will let the prospect share his needs, wants, and values with you. You can lose the sale if you linger in this phase too long and your prospect is on a time deadline, or if you talk too much and bore the prospect. Let the prospect talk three times as much as you. To ensure that this happens, focus on asking open-ended questions.

In phase two, ask open-ended questions one at a time and listen carefully to the responses. Acknowledge his response verbally and nonverbally (as with a head nod) as the person speaks. Remember to allow the prospect to talk three times more than you talk. Most extroverts will find this difficult at first, but when you train yourself to stay quiet and focused, your efforts will pay off handsomely. You learn so much about a person just by listening to *what* they have to say and *how* they say it.

Some examples of good open-ended questions you could ask include:

- What makes your business different from your competitors?
- What are the two most important areas of your business?
- Who are your best clients?
- Who are your worst clients?

Then, as you learned in Chapter 10, mirror back the answers that you hear from the customer, in your own words, to make certain that you've understood what he has said.

You:	"I understand you want a business consultant, but fear that you may lose control of everyday operations. What worries you about losing control of the everyday operations?"
Prospect:	"I need help in getting my team more focused and productive with their time, but I have a hard time trusting anyone else to do what I do."
You:	"Share with me a little more about what would happen if you 'lost control' of this. What is the most important thing about keeping your team focused? What level would you like their focus to be?"

Here you want to ask more specific questions to clarify what your prospect is fearful of in hiring you as a business consultant. Is it money, service, warranty, follow-up, delivery, your accessibility, your experience in solving the problems, or your company's credibility? Find out as specifically as you can what concerns your prospect has.

Information Reflection Phase

In the information reflection phase, you reflect back to your prospects or clients the needs and values they shared with you. You can lose the sale here if you can't get through their resistance or if you failed to pick up on the customers' most important underlying needs and values. If you fail to specifically address their needs by reflecting them back, prospects may not know you understand and care. If you have reflected back their needs and wants and something is not accurate, they will correct you. If your comments are correct, then they will nod their heads or verbally agree with your evaluations.

During the third phase, information reflection, you want to mirror back the most important needs and wants your prospect or customer gave you.

You:	"It seems to me from what you are saying is that . . ." (mention the four or five most important values and wants of your client and how your product or service solves their problem).

If your prospect or customer remains unconvinced at this stage, ask again for the most important part of each statement or concern he brought up. If this reflection goes well, you are ready for the next phase. If the prospect needs more time to make a decision, you may need to come back at a later time and continue this phase then. Be sure to keep in touch and follow up if there is a break between phases three and four.

Signing Phase

Signing is not the close of the sale, since there is no real close. It is simply the point, typically after some negotiation, at which you reach agreement. If you find that you are spending a great deal of time in this phase, then chances are good that you need to build stronger strategies in earlier phases of the selling cycle. The signing phase should be the shortest of the selling cycle—the phase in which your prospect or customer signs on the dotted line. This is not where you "close" the sale; it is only a reinforcement that the prospect or customer feels your products or services will solve his problem. During this phase, you have the opportunity to add extra value by offering a bonus or special customer service. This can make the signing phase even easier and often makes it come more quickly as well.

 Alert

You can lose your prospect if you linger too long in one phase. As you chart the length of each phase in your selling cycle, identify in which phase you experience the most resistance from prospects. You will begin to recognize your selling pattern and be able to identify the hot spots that prevent you from reaching the signing phase.

Chances are you've already shared the price with your prospect by the time you reach phase four. The critical point to remember about price is that the prospect should see both the value of your product or service and the *extra value* that you've provided by bridging his needs and wants with what you have to offer. You just helped him solve a problem, and he wants the product or service! In the negotiation segment of this phase, you added more perceived value to the transaction.

> You: "On top of everything else you get for the $2,000 a month consulting fee, I will add an additional training session for your team and provide personal coaching via e-mail."

You can also tell your prospect how and why you would like to keep providing him with services after the sale.

> You: "I will continue the e-mail coaching for thirty days after our contract expires because I want to make sure that you and your consultants can make the most use of your time and maximize your productivity, particularly after I leave the scene."

Aftercare Phase

The aftercare phase involves staying in communication with your customer. Even if prospects don't buy, you should stay in touch with them, since they may turn into customers at another time. The aftercare phase is when your next sale begins. You have spent the time and the dollars in reaching your customers initially. They now know who you are, what you do, how you do business, what products and services you offer, and that you can help them solve problems. Once a customer has given you his seal of approval by making a purchase, you want to continue to show your appreciation by staying in contact with him on a regular schedule. Not only is he a potential future sale, he is also a source of referrals.

 Fact

Follow-up time is crucial in sales. You have a window of opportunity of approximately forty-eight hours to get back to your prospect or customer in most selling situations. Each day after that that you don't make contact increases your chances of losing out to your competitor. Follow up immediately to keep that window of opportunity open.

The aftercare and follow-up phase is the most important phase for future business. You should already have an automatic system in place for handling future communications. Send your new or returning customer a thank-you note or a gift, and call within a week of signing the contract. Never lose sight of the fact that they spent their time and their dollars with you rather than someone else.

If you omit any phase of the selling cycle, you leave a potentially large hole in your relationship, and it may end sooner than you want. Not only could it cease abruptly, but you may not even know why it happened.

If a prospect calls you after hearing about you from one of her colleagues, you are starting from a position of strength. Referred business is much easier to convert to sales and keep long-term than business found through cold prospecting. The prospect will explain her needs to you, and you will promise to e-mail a price quote. It is here that communication and the sequencing of the phases can break down. Suppose the prospect does not receive your e-mail because her e-mail server was down. If you don't call or e-mail again to make sure she received it, she may think you are ignoring her. Because you were referred, the prospect may give you the benefit of the doubt. She may call you, but if you are too busy to call back, she will get frustrated. Not only will you lose this sale, but the person who referred you will hear about the problems as well. You could lose two customers at once. Take the time to get to know the prospect and understand her needs and concerns. If the prospect is just a "quote" to you, you are missing out on business built by creating relationships.

Ask for the Sale

There are many ways to ask for a sale, and it is your responsibility to learn them well so that you can use them automatically, without even thinking about it. Once you have built a trusting relationship, you're in a good position to ask for the sale. One of the most common core values for people is saving time and gaining the convenience that goes along with it. Being able to also save money in the process is an added bonus.

Then you need to be aware of what the prospect needs. Match the product or service to bottom-line needs and wants of your prospect or customer. Ask questions like: "What about saving money is important for you right now?" You may hear that a couple needs to save for their daughter's wedding and they're strapped for cash. Once you know this, you can reflect it back to them and offer ways you can solve their problem. You might suggest special financing without interest for several months, or offer a payment plan that lets them spread payments over several months. As added value, you may connect them to quality services you know of in the wedding business, saving the couple money, time, and worry.

Believe in What You're Selling

You need to really believe in what you're selling. If you are selling a product or service just for the commission or because it's the only job you think you can get, you may want to re-evaluate your purpose. Life is too short to spend most of your living days with drudgery because you are there to sell and you don't believe in the company, product, or service you're selling.

E ssential

Repeat and referral-based business comes from being honest about the product or service you're selling. You want to solve a customer's problem, not just sell her an item to meet a temporary sales quota if it is not what she wants or needs. If you go the first route, your honesty will lead to repeat business and referrals. If you focus on the second route, you will always be looking for new customers.

You must really believe that what you're selling is the best for your customer. When you are a true partner with your prospects or customers, you won't want to sell them anything just to get a sale. Trying simply to make a sale often backfires. You don't receive many testimonials that way, or obtain customers who become your marketing representatives by telling others to buy your products or services.

Evidence shows that when people are happy with products, services, or a particular sales professional, they will tell two or three people about it, but when they have a bad experience, they tell more than ten people about it.

Talk about Price

At some point it will be time to talk about price. When you have good rapport with your prospect or customer and he is agreeing to everything you say and talking as though he will use these products or services, then it's time to ask how he would like to pay for it. If his reaction to this question is to stop short and act as if he's suddenly concerned that he can't afford the purchase, it's important to go back to phase three—the information reflection phase—and find out the deeper reasons why he needs or wants your products or services.

Discuss the Benefits

All sales are potentially time-sensitive. Speak to prospects as though they already own the product or service, and explain how it solves their problems. A successful sales strategy is to help your prospects or customers see the benefits that they'll get from buying your products or services. Give them specific examples of how their lives will function differently and better if they make this purchase.

Show your prospects that you are available for them, making it convenient for them. Give them names of others who have used your services and the *results* of these partnerships. The real proof of your effectiveness lies in the quality of your products or services. Products that provide real results lead to sales.

Take Action to Close the Sale

Many times during the close you will hear the prospect or customer say, "Okay, let's do it," or something similar, to let you know that she is ready to finish the deal. But if you find that your customer is not asking you to finish the deal, you may want to take the lead to get there. Choose the approach that works best for the customer's particular situation.

You may need to ask such questions as:

- What needs to happen for you to move forward on this?
- What can I do to help you move forward on this?
- How would you like to pay for this?

The prospect or customer may need more information before she is ready to buy. If so, find it and get back to her as soon as possible. The more time that elapses, the more likely it is that she will move on to your competitor.

Talk as If the Sale Is Already Closed

By the time you're ready to sign the contract, you will find that you have been talking as if the deal is done. You have offered the prospect added value, created a trusting relationship, shown your professionalism and interest, and presented solutions that fill needs, wants, and core values. At this point, your prospect wants to know when she can start using the product or service. If you find in the conversation that she is uneasy, that she objects to the price or anything else, that is a signal that something has been lacking in the process of completing the sale. You may not have uncovered her real needs and core values, or you still need to explain how your products and services can address those needs and values to solve her problems.

Paint the Picture of Successful Closings in Your Mind

All your senses are extraordinarily strong when you are making decisions. Successful athletes often spend a great deal of time visualizing their performances before competitions. Visualization is becoming increasingly popular as a powerful influence in health and healing. Golf great Jack Nicklaus once said, "I never hit a shot, not even in practice, without having a very sharp, in-focus picture of it in my head. It's like a color movie." Sales professionals can also benefit enormously from visualization, but only if they focus on specific parts of the sales process. It's not enough to visualize something as vague as "having an excellent sales year." You have to picture yourself and your prospects performing specific actions.

Visualize yourself being fully knowledgeable about your products or services, explaining their primary benefits for different demographic groups. Visualize yourself going through the sales cycle asking open-ended questions and listening intently to the answers, picking up on both verbal and nonverbal cues. As you visualize asking the questions, see yourself finding the deepest level of importance for your clients who are making the purchase. Visualize yourself holding the signed agreement, and picture how pleased the prospect or customer is. See yourself doing follow-up as part of your aftercare and transforming the prospect into a loyal repeat customer and positive word-of-mouth marketing rep for you.

 Fact

Successful sales professionals use visualization as part of their selling arsenal. Most top athletes, excellent speakers, and other extraordinary professionals say that they visualize every part of their game or presentation before they start performing. Sports psychologists use visualization as an important tool to help improve athletes' performance.

Visualization works best when you do it regularly. If you try to cram it in before an important meeting, it will be less effective. (But even cramming it in is better than not doing it at all.) Lastly, help your prospects and customers to visualize what their personal or work life will be like with the product or service you provide.

The Last Thing to Close

How many times have you bought a product or a service that you originally thought was too expensive? What made you spend the additional money? What affected you when making up your mind and spurred you to spend more than you originally budgeted for? If you take a few minutes to answer these questions for yourself, focusing on specific situations, it will become clear why price is not always the decisive factor when buying.

Chances are great that the price of your products or services were brought up fairly early in the selling process. Your prospect probably compared prices earlier or came in because of a low price you advertised. Price is typically usually discussed in phase one (introduction) or phase two (values and needs information) of the selling cycle. But often the price is not the most important part of a sale, especially if you can show how valuable the product or service is to your prospect or customer.

The more you delve into price, the more you see that, while it is important, it is perhaps not as important as you thought at first. This is especially true if you have prepared for the sale and developed a trusting relationship with the prospect or customer. Quality, customer service, and relationships are factors that can far outweigh price when a customer makes a decision to buy.

Chapter 21

The Ethics of Selling

The money you accumulate in your business gives you wonderful opportunities to do good deeds. You also have the greater opportunity to bring prosperity and health to your community. Younger generations are placing a priority on cleaning up the messes made by previous generations of people and businesses. It is an awesome task, but one that must be done. Contributing to your community will not only give you personal satisfaction but will send a message to your prospects and customers that you are interested in more than just money.

The Legacy You Will Be Remembered For

How people respond to money can reflect their strengths, weaknesses, and prejudices. Issues with money affect how fairly people work with others, how carefully they clean up environmental abuses, and how thoughtfully they solve health issues. Your natural instincts might be to maximize profit at any cost, but your conscience will tell you to balance that with other things that matter, too.

Money can be a positive force in your business and in your life. How you use it determines part of your legacy. To leave a positive legacy, it is important to establish your own internal business code of ethics. You may decide that you are willing to work only for a socially responsible company. You may give to local charities and be remembered for the change you help facilitate in your community. You may contribute more globally and make a change in the world.

Many large firms are talking about values, both internally with their employees, and externally with their clients. These companies are helping to promote a strong code of ethics all around the world. As more and more sales reps make conscious decisions to work only for socially responsible companies, those companies gain a competitive edge in hiring. And as more and more people choose to do business only with socially responsible companies, being socially responsible gives those companies a competitive edge for attracting customers, too. That is quite an economic and ecological statement! Firms are focusing on internal business codes of ethics, particularly after the alarming number of large businesses that have gone bankrupt in disgrace in the last few years. They are doing it because it is good business to be ethical.

Unethical Behavior and Sales

What are the costs of doing business irresponsibly? Studies show that it harms sales. People don't like to buy from companies that act unethically. According to a survey conducted by Wirthlin Worldwide in 2003, 80 percent of people choose to purchase a company's products or services based partly on their sense of the company's ethics.

Social irresponsibility can destroy goodwill and lower productivity. "It takes years to build a good business reputation, but one false move can destroy it overnight," says Edson W. Spencer, the former chairman of Honeywell. Kenneth C. Frazier, the chairman of the Ethics Resource Center and vice president and general counsel of Merck, says, "Nobody should have any doubts of the linkages between poor ethics in the workplace and low productivity." The 2003 National Business Ethics Survey showed that lack of trust in the workplace increases stress and reduces output.

Retention and recruiting is hampered if a company isn't acting ethically. People prefer to work at companies that have good character. Ethical firms attract top talent more easily. They also minimize turnover, thereby keeping qualified employees and wasting less time training new employees. Companies with the highest employee retention keep customers the most effectively, too. Customers usually follow their sales rep, and if a sales rep leaves because a company is unethical, the customers will hear about it.

Being socially responsible is an effective employee motivator. Studies show that motivated employees enjoy their jobs more and are more productive as a result. When you establish and *use* your business code of ethics, it becomes simpler to do what's right rather than what's easy, because you are following your code of values. Some business people believe you can't be socially responsible and make a profit, but that's a myth. The large number of socially responsible companies that are extremely profitable are a testament to that.

 Fact

A fivefold increase in customer retention typically boosts profits by 25 to 100 percent. Companies looking to boost profits by keeping their work teams intact have a higher success rate than those with higher employee turnover.

What's Right Versus What's Easy

It is socially responsible for businesses to manufacture their products or perform their services in a way that does not introduce toxins into the environment. As a sales rep, working for a company that follows ethical business practices will make your sales job easier. Companies that publicly give away a percentage of their profits or are otherwise known for working for social change are the companies you should target in your job search. Innovative, high-quality products, economic success, and social change are all tied together.

Bringing Character to Everything

No matter what type of sales you're in, you can make a difference, even as just one person. The power of one truly is remarkable! Your personal ethics and your personal social responsibility can increase your sales exponentially with each prospect. As one customer learns your business acumen and tells another, that one customer becomes two. As they learn and tell others, those two become four, and four become eight, and your sales continue to increase.

If you are a sales rep for a small company or if you are an independent contractor, you can still show your prospects your own code of social responsibility. You may donate a portion of your sales locally or to your customers' favorite charity. You may spend time picking up litter or helping out in the schools. You may serve in a soup kitchen or work at your local church or synagogue.

Social responsibility plays a powerful role in the success of a business. Successful direct selling and multilevel selling companies use this to their benefit. Respect for nature and sound business practices are integral to your business, shareholders, customers, and the people you serve.

Alert

Many socially irresponsible companies and sales professionals misjudge the level of scrutiny they are under, thinking that because few are paying attention today, no one will look back to examine their actions tomorrow.

Some companies may feel pressured into doing the right thing, because of potential government restrictions, the risk of bad publicity, or worse yet, the chance of lawsuits. They may be acting unethically while no one is looking, but changing their ways as soon as they feel they could get caught. They believe they are being practical, when in fact they are on a slippery slope. Small, unnoticed offenses today can lead to bigger and bigger offenses tomorrow, until major crimes can become standard operating procedure. When researching the companies you want to work for, be sure that their ethics come from within rather than from outside pressure. If they go above and beyond the minimum standard requirements, if they are socially responsible because they want to be, you will find an environment conducive to your success.

Punishing Unethical Companies

One of the most effective ways to change a company is for people to change how they spend their money. Health-conscious supermarkets have higher profit margins than conventional ones, and the demand for hybrid cars, which require less dependence on oil, has soared. In response to the increasing rates of obesity in children and adults, food manufacturers are changing the ingredients they use in their food. As a sales rep, your ability to effect change comes from your willingness to represent the companies whose policies you support. With no representation by sales reps, companies that act irresponsibly would have to face a decision to either change or fail.

Such changes are happening today in many industries, as a result of people voting with their pocketbooks, good sales reps refusing to work for companies they disagree with, and reports in the media about shady business practices.

Choosing a Company to Work For

The theory of cognitive dissonance was first proposed by Leon Festinger in 1956. The theory of cognitive dissonance says that when you choose an action that conflicts with your values, you create internal dissonance. To get rid of it, you'll likely change your perception to condone the action. This phenomenon certainly occurs in business. If you work for a company or a boss who does business in a way you consider unethical and you continue to work there, you will find that you start to change your perceptions so that you no longer see the company's actions as unethical, you justify staying there because of the amount of money you're making, you start to believe that "all companies do business like this," or you devise rationalizations such as "but they give so much money to charity."

One of the quickest ways to lose positive energy is to work in a company whose business ethics run counter to yours. If you do not share the values of the company you work for, you need to make some changes, and fast. By working in a company contrary to your own beliefs, your beliefs will start to erode away as you justify your choices.

Partnering with Nonprofits

It is important that companies and particularly sales reps hook up and partner with nonprofits. It is the right thing to do, and it helps others less fortunate. It demonstrates the ethics of the company and the sales rep. It works as an employee recruitment and retention tool as well as a morale booster.

The Law of Prosperity states that the more prosperous you become, the more prosperous those around you become. Similarly, the Law of Attraction says that like attracts like, so good deeds beget other good deeds, and negative deeds beget other negative ones. If you act badly, you'll attract others who act badly, and you never know when they'll act badly toward you. By working for the better good, the good will come to you as well.

The Truth Works

One of the most important characteristics a prospect or customer looks for when establishing a relationship with a salesperson is integrity. They want to support businesses and professionals that take personal responsibility and social responsibility seriously. There are certain imperatives that most of us believe are simply the right thing to do. Some of these include taking responsibility to protect and use our natural resources; to keep our forests, water, and air clean; to protect and help other people and animals.

Take responsibility to repair anything you break or damage, including a person's self-esteem or reputation. Take responsibility for your behavior, actions, and words, and take responsibility for living a balanced life. Take responsibility for rectifying your mistakes immediately. If you realize there is an accounting error on the books, be truthful and rectify it.

 Fact

Positive reinforcement and showing appreciation to your employees or vendors is more powerful as a motivator than negative reinforcement. Studies show that expressing positive comments to your employees and showing your appreciation for what they do increases their productivity.

What type of sales professional do you want to become? You are in the driver's seat, and only you can make the powerful decision of what company you will work for. Make the choice that you and your customers will be proud of and that will make a positive difference in their lives today and for the generations yet to come.

Chapter 22

Using the Internet to Bring in More Sales

Sales reps who embrace the Internet—learning about it, using it to its fullest, and creating interactive material on it—will exceed their expectations as well as their customers'. The Internet increases the potential for excellence in client satisfaction, client loyalty, cross-selling functionality, and follow-up capabilities in almost any career field. The Internet is a catchall for honest comments, good and bad, about products, services, and customer service. Positive comments can help you increase sales, but negative comments can ruin your business. The Internet has raised the bar for customer service.

Exceeding Expectations via the Internet

Because habits are so ingrained, it takes a lot for people to change them, whether they're lifestyle or buying habits. You'll never know how happy or satisfied your customers are unless you interact with them and find out. The best and most straightforward approach is to ask them. Create an online survey that you can send to customers after they've purchased your product to capture their level of satisfaction with the product and the sales process. This level of interactivity encourages customer loyalty.

Unless you have asked your customers if they are happy, you won't know how they feel. Many sales reps only find out that their customers are not happy or pleased with their products, services, or follow-up after the customer leaves and stops doing business with them. It is four times more expensive to recapture customers than to keep them onboard for the long haul. Keeping in touch and asking for feedback is paramount in keeping customers.

Responding to Customers

Once you know how happy or unhappy a prospect or customer is, it is important to both acknowledge her response and do something about it. This applies whether she is happy or unhappy. The worst word-of-mouth advertising usually comes from unhappy prospects or customers, but no word-of-mouth advertising comes from happy customers if they don't remember who you are. The bottom line is to do whatever you can to keep your customer happy and keep in touch with them to ensure that they remember you. When you do, you will develop loyalty and referrals.

If buyers say they are unhappy for any reason, respond to their comments and do what is necessary to rectify the situation. If someone says, "Yes, I am happy with my products or services," then offer him a special discount on another purchase or offer something else of value to say thank you for his business. This makes him an even happier customer.

If a customer says he is not happy with your service, the follow-up, or even with the product, find a way to compensate him or offer to let him try a new product or service for the same price.

Repeat Sales

You can use the Internet to cross-sell—that is, to sell customers products and services that are similar to or related to ones they've bought previously or to sell them products that have been bought by other people who bought the same thing they did. Technology such as your customer relationship management software can track which products or services a customer bought and help you continue to market to these customers with other lines of similar products or services.

The Internet has made follow-up so much faster, simpler, and time-efficient. No matter where you are, you can shoot off a quick note to someone you just met or a thank you to a customer. Sales professionals don't want to bother their prospects or customers, so they may be tempted to go awhile without contact, but you will never bother people if you have something of value to share. Send the customers in your database a photo of a new product, information on specials on certain products, discounts that are good for a short specified time, timely articles, or numerous other offers of value or real information.

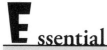

With the Internet, you are as big as your mind allows you to be. Even brand-new businesses can achieve a professional Web presence that's on par with that of much larger, more established companies. A professionally built Web site gives the small entrepreneur, the large company, and the fledgling sales rep the same chances at capturing customers online.

If there is one common area where sales professionals lose clients, it is in follow-up. Although follow-up takes time and can sometimes seem to be a waste of time, it must be a large part of your marketing plan. The Internet lets you do it very efficiently and effectively and as a result increases your sales performance potential.

The Internet and Sales Performance

Keep in mind these five critical elements of creating your Internet presence: your mindset, your Web site, your database, your online community, and opt-in features. All of these elements should be addressed in every Web site that you develop. Your mindset today needs to be, "Think globally." The more people know about you and your products and services, the more sales income you will generate. Think big and your sales will follow.

Online reports, online magazines, blogs, and podcasts have mushroomed into thriving sources focused on every topic imaginable. In today's information age, your customers and colleagues are hungry for more knowledge, as long as they perceive it as valuable. Today more than ever, knowledge is power.

You need to decide how to portray yourself and what message you want to convey on your Web site. Think of your Internet site as a twenty-four-hour-a-day selling tool. What is it about your product that people want? What do your clients say about you? If you don't know, ask: You can say simply, "What is important about my services to you?" Include those services on your Web site. Offer good content that answers questions and solves customers' problems.

Web Sites

There are two types of Web sites to consider: static and dynamic. Most people have static Web sites, in which the information on them does not change until the owner or Webmaster edits the site. These Web sites get all the information needed across to the visitors and allows customers to contact you as well. They're the quickest and cheapest Web sites to develop. Many of the functions of a static Web site are limited and not automated. You can add software to help a static site become a bit more interactive. For instance, by adding shopping cart software, you can expand the interactivity of your Web site to make it possible for visitors to purchase products and services online. Establishing a community and collecting the names of new visitors who buy or subscribe to an online newsletter or download an e-book adds another interactive element and is not as expensive as building a dynamic Web site.

A dynamic Web site provides complete interactivity with your visitors using programming that allows visitors to submit information, create profiles, do database searches, or do anything else you can offer that would be useful to your customers. Dynamic sites can provide video streaming and voice-activated tools as well as autoresponders (which generate e-mails automatically, such as to confirm a subscription to a mailing list) and much more. If you have the interest and the money, and if you believe you can benefit from using fully interactive technology on your Web site, then create this type of site. When you know who you are to your customers and the importance of the value you bring to them, you are in an excellent position to communicate this information on your Web site.

 Fact

Consumers today are very sophisticated about technology, and they crave information to help them solve all kinds of problems. Provide worthwhile information so that your Web site visitors keep coming back. The more they check out your Web site, the greater chance you have of selling them products or services.

Customize Your Database

Stay in contact regularly and consistently with the people in your database. Create a Web site with a shopping cart that lets your prospects and customers buy online. This interactivity also allows you to communicate more closely with them. Customize your database by developing specific categories. There's much more to creating a database than just putting in a prospect's name, address, phone number, and e-mail. You can add categories that let you keep track of a variety of details: gender, specific generation by age, new parents, just married, homeowners under two years, homeowners for over ten years, condo dwellers, socioeconomic level, hobbies, notes about where or how you met them, geographical location, and many more. The more specific you are, the better your database can act as a customer relationship marketing tool. And that is priceless!

What is the sales performance potential? The better you know your prospects and customers, the more they will connect with you, and you will start to have a loyal following. Remember that your visitors will start purchasing after a few visits to your Web site, but rarely the first time. Be patient. It takes seven "hits" or views in regular advertising channels for someone to think about buying your product or service.

Creating Community

People crave community. They function best when they're a part of a community rather than isolated. Developing a community by hosting message boards on your Web site is an excellent way to create interactivity between you and your clients. It also allows them to connect with others who have similar problems, or learn new ways to approach or use your products and services. Creating communities and message boards encourages your customers to interact with each other. Their brainstorming can help you to learn new ways of serving them.

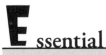

E ssential

All communities have needs, and satisfying these needs translates into good customer service and more products and services sold. The most effective strategy here is to "capture" all your online visitors. These visitors are prescreened, and chances are they are interested in what you are selling.

What is the sales potential in creating an online community? By encouraging others to join a group, you are inviting your customers a little closer into your life and the lives of others with similar interests and concerns. In effect you are saying, "I care" and "Let's share with others what we've learned so that others can benefit from these products or services."

You can also give your customers and colleagues a window into your life by posting your schedule on your Web site. You can easily share your schedule with those you do business with, just by setting up an Internet calendar. This can be useful for someone whose sales territory, for example, covers a few hundred miles or several cities. Your online calendar can alert your colleagues, vendors, and customers when you'll be in their area. Displaying your schedule publicly has two other advantages: It forces you to plan in advance, and it helps you keep your commitment to travel to specific areas. Your colleagues, vendors, and customers can simply go online to see your schedule and know where you'll be on any given day.

Opt-In Features

Don't spam visitors to your site by sending them unwanted e-mails. You don't want to add to the avalanche of unsolicited pitches people receive every day by e-mail. Instead, offer a feature that lets visitors opt in to an e-mail list. Develop an opt-in space on your Web site that gives new visitors a reason to provide you with their e-mail addresses. Ask for just first names, as research has shown you're more apt to get an accurate e-mail address that way. Also ask for their primary e-mail address, or you may get their "junk mail" address. And offer something of perceived value to prompt your visitor to give you their e-mail address. You may want to make a list of your customers' top ten questions or concerns and offer it as a download free for opting in.

Alert

You must offer something of perceived value before you will have prospects opting in to your Web site, podcast, or blog. The more good content you have in the form of e-books, reports, and surveys that you offer for free, the higher chance you have of getting your visitors to give you their e-mail addresses and sign in.

The e-mail addresses you collect become your communication and advertising vehicle to sell your products and services to a niche market. You will have a higher sell-through to people who are already interested in what you are selling.

Partnering with Related Web Sites

Partnering with other Web sites is another good sales strategy. It is your job to determine which Web sites and professionals are similar enough to complement you but different enough that they don't siphon business away. You want to offer "combination buys," if possible.

Partnering on the Internet allows for you to connect with other professionals on a much larger scale than you could alone and gives you access to more contacts instantly. Focus on partnering with those Web sites that have a minimum of 5,000 on their mailing lists. You will create a larger pool to which to sell your products and services with less effort.

Affiliate programs allow you to be introduced to the prospects and clients of other professionals, and act as an Internet version of word-of-mouth advertising. You receive instant introductions to mostly prescreened and warm leads.

There are several types of affiliate programs. The most important goal in partnering with affiliate Web sites is to create a large and niche-driven customer base. The more carefully chosen affiliates you partner with, the more viral your marketing becomes. (Viral marketing is similar to the spread of a cold: It goes from one person to another and then another, and so on.)

You can also offer advertising on your site, in which others pay you to place their ads. You can contribute articles to other Web sites in your field or associated fields. You can interview centers of influence in your area of expertise, and they can interview you in turn, and post the interviews on your respective Web sites, podcasts, or blogs.

Teleseminars, discussed in earlier chapters, are online seminars that usually last about sixty minutes. The speaker typically gives a presentation that lasts approximately forty-five minutes and then answers questions from the participants for the remaining fifteen. These are an excellent service to offer for free so that others have an opportunity to hear you before they purchase a course, an e-book, a book, or other products or services from you. You might even consider recording your teleseminars and putting them on CDs as additional product to sell.

You can't beat "word-of-Net" promotions. In these programs, other professionals or businesses promote your products or services in their e-newsletters.

Increasing Access to Information

Prospects and customers want to do business with people who have excellent knowledge about their products or services coupled with integrity. Often prospects and customers pass on a sale because the sales rep didn't have enough information about the product to answer all their questions. And this may be one reason—beyond time efficiency—that online sales have become so popular. Prospects have the information about the products and services at their fingertips, and they can request and receive more instantly. In addition, the Internet makes it possible for prospects to comparison shop based on product features, benefits, and price—all with just a few clicks.

E ssential

Send out an e-newsletter to everyone in your database once a month. It can be a business-style letter one month and a personal-style letter the next. Vary the type of content you include, such as helpful tips, recommendations, and other information.

It's important to make your Web site stand out and make it easy to navigate so that prospects and customers will stay connected with it. The longer someone is connected to your site, the more likely they will buy from you. How, then, do you as a sales professional in your industry stand out? Use the Internet to reinforce your branding and move ahead of the competition.

Creating an E-Newsletter

We live in an age in which we have easy access to vast amounts of information. There has never been a better time to create brand awareness for you and your business. Yet this access creates its own problem: the information overload people feel from all corners of their lives, from ads on cars to billboards to ad sponsors on Internet sites to ads in movie theaters. So you must communicate your message in a way that is as focused, consistent, and repetitive as possible. One excellent way to do this is through your own e-newsletter.

E-Newsletter Formats

E-newsletters tend to come in two major styles: magazine-style layout and plain text layout. Magazine-style layouts display graphics, typically using the HTML formatting language. They may resemble a magazine page, showing several topics at a glance. The most effective ones display one interesting lead paragraph per article on the front page and include a link that readers can click on to read the rest of the story.

Plain text layouts, on the other hand, are also effective, especially when you focus on giving good, solid information to your readers. This style works best for giving how-to tips and suggesting Web sites that will help your readers find additional information. It also requires less time and expertise to create and lets you send much smaller files that don't take long to download.

Content

Regardless of format, all successful e-newsletters have certain traits in common. They include a short synopsis of all topics that are covered within them and a link that leads to the full article. The focus is on the author's (in this case, the sales professional's) business and reinforces the author's credibility and knowledge. And the newsletter focuses ways the author can acquire new prospects and new Web site visitors. E-newsletters or e-zines are excellent marketing strategies as well as a useful means of staying in contact with prospects and clients.

Developing a content-filled and interactive e-newsletter is an excellent nonintrusive marketing tool for staying in touch with your prospects and customers. Make sure you show your personality in the e-zine. Make it friendly and personable. People crave being recognized and acknowledged. This has led marketers in a variety of fields to develop individualized programs and services that speak directly to customers. This opportunity is a sales rep's dream!

E-zines can be vehicles for introducing new products or services; a means of working smarter rather than harder by communicating new programs, products, and services to a large group at once; and a way to engage your target markets interactively.

Web Sites for Sales Professionals

Developing, creating, and marketing your Web site is not difficult if you have the resources to help you through it. Information truly is power in this case. The sales rep who takes advantage of available resources to help produce and market their products and services in a new technological era will reach their goals that much sooner. Some Web sites that can help you get started using the Internet to boost your sales career are:

- *www.salescentral.com:* Provides excellent articles for sales professionals monthly.
- *www.nelson-motivation.com*: Offers excellent ideas on how to motivate employees, show appreciation to your customers, and so much more.
- *www.bizweb2000.com*: Offers good advice for turning your Web site and your brand into online sales.

You are the driver in creating your Internet presence. Learn as much as you can about the Internet and how it can help you achieve your sales goals and target the most appropriate segment of the population for your service or product. Practice writing sales copy and creating reports and mini-surveys for your prospects and customers. Create your Web site, give it your personality and uniqueness, and make it count!

Chapter 23

Tying It All Together

One of your goals is to prepare for a highly successful and gratifying professional sales career. This process begins with giving it your all and investing in your education and character. Planning and organization are vital for achieving success and using time management principles to increase productivity and time efficiency and reduce stress. You never know when your persistence will pay off handsomely—the success you truly have worked for may only be an arm's length away!

Getting Ready for a Sales Career

Once you've decided on your career path, give it your all. You spend so many hours at work that it only makes sense to use this time pursuing your highest values and goals and reinforcing these with your behavior. Research continues to find that true grit—persistence and drive—is more important than talent in achieving success. There is also a link between determination and optimism, since the perception of a positive future encourages persistence, and determination improves your record of success, which itself makes you more optimistic about future successes.

Your thoughts reflect your attitude, and your attitude reflects your success. Your feelings and thoughts are transparent and are revealed visibly in your behavior. It is important for you to become aware of the consistency or inconsistency of your thoughts and actions. This is where real change can occur.

Fact

Research shows that talent takes a back seat to persistence and drive. Successful companies share in common a persistence and drive to turn their entrepreneurial spirit into thriving businesses. You need to earmark focused time to be productive and work toward the success you desire.

Guiding Your Thoughts

Psychologists have said for years: If you want to change your actions, then change the way you think. That is why it is so important to take time every day to focus on your goals, positive thoughts, attitudes, and actions. Eventually, your subconscious will begin to believe your thoughts if they are consistent, and slowly you can change the negative ideas you were holding on to into more positive thoughts that are more in line with the way you want to communicate and act. The more consistent your feelings, thoughts, and actions, the less stress you will feel, the less energy you will lose in everyday activities and communications, and the more you have to give it your all and reach each of your goals.

If you give it your all, you will feel your work has purpose and will make the most of your time with activities that matter to you. You become more knowledgeable in your field and more comfortable with what you're doing and how you do it. Your relationships at work and at home are stronger, and you become internally motivated to achieve your goals. In fact, reaching your goals becomes a self-fulfilling prophecy.

Invest in Yourself

If you don't invest in you, who will? Become familiar with your buyer motivations, the top ten benefits of your products or services, and ways to go beyond consumer expectations, all while maintaining integrity in all your business dealings. The way people perceive you colors the way they respond to you. If others think that you don't know your products and services, that you look unkempt, or that you often criticize others, your prospects and customers may respond to you with less respect. And when others treat you with disrespect you usually feel it down to your bones.

As with many things, you control the factors that lead to a successful sale. If others are reacting less than positively to your actions, it will show—in the form of fewer sales. It behooves you to take the time and energy to prepare yourself better. In fact, the very act of picking up this book shows that you are taking the necessary steps toward developing a highly successful sales career.

Plan for and Visualize Your Success

The more you feed and nurture your subconscious mind with what you want, the better chance you will get it. If you picture yourself as successful, living a life rich with good health, loving relationships, and meaningful work, your subconscious mind will start to internalize these thoughts and you'll find it easier to take action.

Visualization can enhance this process, so visualize building and maintaining strong relationships based on integrity and follow-up as anchors. See yourself effortlessly finding the common bond between you and your customer, building and maintaining the relationship, following up, and doing what it takes to exceed your customer's expectations.

Alert

It is difficult to think one way and act another. Focus on viewing every transaction in a positive light. You have the ability to change your negative evaluations to positive ones just by changing your perception of the event or transaction. Looking at things and situations in a negative light will hamper your efforts to reach your goals.

It is no longer enough just to meet your prospects' and customers' expectations if you want to pull ahead of the pack. You must find ways to exceed their needs and wants every time. If you don't know how, simply ask your customers in person, by mail, or by e-mail. They will be more than happy to share with you several ways you can do it. Always be thinking: What is one more thing I can do for my prospect or customer to exceed her expectations?

One of the most effective and easiest ways to exceed your prospects' and customers' expectations is to ask them what they want. Create your own marketing campaign based on the answers you receive.

Maximizing Your Talents

Your talents are what you make of them. If you have a passion for something, chances are you can develop the talent that it takes to reach a new dimension of professionalism and competency. You need to encourage your internal passions to shine through. This is part of your unique branding in your field. Seeking your passions usually helps reveal your true talents. This passion is also reflected in enthusiasm for what you are doing. Enthusiasm is contagious and serves as an added value in the selling process.

If you are patient and pay attention to which activities, places, and words resonate with you, you'll move closer to focusing on your true passion. Everyone has a passion, and it's your job to discover what truly excites you. Find your natural talent and use it in your sales career.

Think outside the box and be willing to create new things. Entrepreneurs have developed some of the best-known businesses today by thinking differently. In fact, many highly successful small businesses discovered an unmet need through personal experience or frustration in not finding the product or service they were searching for. The baby stroller used by jogging parents arose from exasperation—its inventor simply couldn't find such a product, so he made one.

One of the main objectives of your sales career is solving problems. Consumers love to hear the following phrase from sales professionals: "No problem, I can help you." The more benefits you can offer your prospects and customers, beyond meeting their core values in the buying process, the more satisfied customers you will have. And these customers will become your virtual marketing department by giving you word-of-mouth advertising.

Rejection Is Not a Personal Attack

One of the most difficult parts of sales is the number of nos you receive, particularly at the start of your career. How do you keep going back when you're hearing more nos than yeses? You must believe in the products or services that you are selling. Try to match your products and services with the specific clients, and become knowledgeable about your products and services. Remember to create a relationship even though you may have lost the sale. You will only feel bad about you receiving a no if you give yourself permission to.

E ssential

Become familiar with ways to add value to your products or services, including no-risk guarantees. Read through your favorite newspapers and magazines and write down all the different types of no-risk guarantees being offered to customers. Identify those that you can use in your specialty area.

There are many ways to cut the chance of hearing no—and they all start with asking open-ended questions that get customers to share their core values, needs, and wants. You want to find out what is important to them. Once they give you the answer, delve further and ask them what is important about the answer they just shared with you. Your best aids here are listening more than speaking and focusing on what they are communicating nonverbally through body language, tone of voice, and inflection. If you see inconsistency between what is being said and how it is said, further pinpoint the inconsistency and figure out how you can best help your customer solve his problem.

Think Big and Do It!

One of the major ways to think big is to plan big. Again, think outside the box. Where can you find a new niche for your products or services? Identify the similarities and differences among your existing prospects and clients, then look for other markets with those similarities. When you have identified these markets, think big! With the Internet and today's electronic technology, you can be and act much bigger than you would have thought possible only a few years ago!

Remember that psychographics like buying habits and lifestyle changes are just as important today as demographics such as sex, location, and marital status. For example, the baby boomer generation is extending midlife well into what was considered "old age" only five to ten years ago. Your selling strategies must reflect these new lifestyle changes.

Build up your team of advisors and your team of virtual assistants and tangible assistants, and review their contributions often. The best aid to managing anything is being able to measure results. Without good systems for measuring and completing goals, it becomes more difficult to manage yourself, your business, and your team members.

People think in terms of the space before them and fill the space that they have. So think BIG and let that "space" be huge so you can fill it up entirely.

 Fact

Everyone is capable of exceeding their expectations. As you develop your business and marketing plans, go back over your first round of ideas and strategies and make your goals 50 percent larger. When you have focus and a roadmap to get there, your persistence, motivation, and discipline takes over from there.

Think of all the times you have done things above and beyond what you thought was possible. Think of friends or others you admire who have achieved more than they believed they could. You just have to think big at the beginning.

Never Give Up

When you think about the people you consider truly successful, you can see clearly how many of them simply never gave up. Jack Canfield and Mark Victor Hansen never gave up in getting their first *Chicken Soup for the Soul* book published, and they received over 100 rejections by publishers!

Surround yourself with people who validate you and your talents. This support net can help you stay in the game much longer and be more tenacious than you would have ever believed. As an added bonus, their generous and helpful spirits will help boost your energy and motivation. With vigor, purpose, and focus, you create your own high-powered engine to power your sales career to success.

80-20 Prospect Sheet

Prospect	Products/Services	Demographics

Date _____   Tier 1

Psychographics   Follow-up

_____ _____ _____

_____ _____ _____

_____ _____ _____

_____ _____ _____

_____ _____ _____

_____ _____ _____

_____ _____ _____

_____ _____ _____

_____ _____ _____

_____ _____ _____

_____ _____ _____

_____ _____ _____

_____ _____ _____

_____ _____ _____

_____ _____ _____

_____ _____ _____

_____ _____ _____

_____ _____ _____

80-20 Prospect Sheet

Prospect	Products/Services	Demographics
_____	_____	_____
_____	_____	_____
_____	_____	_____
_____	_____	_____
_____	_____	_____
_____	_____	_____
_____	_____	_____
_____	_____	_____
_____	_____	_____
_____	_____	_____
_____	_____	_____
_____	_____	_____
_____	_____	_____
_____	_____	_____
_____	_____	_____
_____	_____	_____
_____	_____	_____

Date _____   Tier 2

Psychographics   Follow-up

_____ _____ _____

_____ _____ _____

_____ _____ _____

_____ _____ _____

_____ _____ _____

_____ _____ _____

_____ _____ _____

_____ _____ _____

_____ _____ _____

_____ _____ _____

_____ _____ _____

_____ _____ _____

_____ _____ _____

_____ _____ _____

_____ _____ _____

_____ _____ _____

_____ _____ _____

_____ _____ _____

80-20 Prospect Sheet

Prospect	Products/Services	Demographics

Date _____   Tier 3

Psychographics   Follow-up

_____ _____ _____
_____ _____ _____
_____ _____ _____
_____ _____ _____
_____ _____ _____
_____ _____ _____
_____ _____ _____
_____ _____ _____
_____ _____ _____
_____ _____ _____
_____ _____ _____
_____ _____ _____
_____ _____ _____
_____ _____ _____
_____ _____ _____
_____ _____ _____
_____ _____ _____
_____ _____ _____
_____ _____ _____
_____ _____ _____

Customer Service Follow-Up Sheet

Name of Customer: _____

Date Serviced: _____

Description: _____

_____

_____

Response: _____

_____

_____

Name of Customer: _____

Date Serviced: _____

Description: _____

_____

_____

Response: _____

_____

_____

Name of Customer: _____

Date Serviced: _____

Description: _____

_____

_____

Response: _____

_____

_____

Name of Customer: _____

Date Serviced: _____

Description: _____

_____

_____

Response: _____

_____

_____

Name of Customer: _____

Date Serviced: _____

Description: _____

_____

_____

Response: _____

_____

_____

Name of Customer: _____

Date Serviced: _____

Description: _____

_____

_____

Response: _____

_____

_____

Customer Service Follow-Up Sheet

Name of Customer: _____

Date Serviced: _____

Description: _____

_____

_____

Response: _____

_____

_____

Name of Customer: _____

Date Serviced: _____

Description: _____

_____

_____

Response: _____

_____

_____

Name of Customer: _____

Date Serviced: _____

Description: _____

_____

_____

Response: _____

_____

_____

Name of Customer: _____

Date Serviced: _____

Description: _____

_____

_____

Response: _____

_____

_____

Name of Customer: _____

Date Serviced: _____

Description: _____

_____

_____

Response: _____

_____

_____

Name of Customer: _____

Date Serviced: _____

Description: _____

_____

_____

Response: _____

_____

_____

Customer Call Follow-Up Sheet

Prospect's Name: _____

Date: _____

Products/Services Required: _____

_____

_____

Description of Conversation: _____

_____

_____

Date of follow-up call: _____

Next contact date: _____

Prospect's Name: _____

Date: _____

Products/Services Required: _____

_____

_____

Description of Conversation: _____

_____

_____

Date of follow-up call: _____

Next contact date: _____

Prospect's Name: _____

Date: _____

Products/Services Required: _____

_____

_____

Description of Conversation: _____

_____

_____

Date of follow-up call: _____

Next contact date: _____

Prospect's Name: _____

Date: _____

Products/Services Required: _____

_____

_____

Description of Conversation: _____

_____

_____

Date of follow-up call: _____

Next contact date: _____

Prospect's Name: _____

Date: _____

Products/Services Required: _____

_____

_____

Description of Conversation: _____

_____

_____

Date of follow-up call: _____

Next contact date: _____

Prospect's Name: _____

Date: _____

Products/Services Required: _____

_____

_____

Description of Conversation: _____

_____

_____

Date of follow-up call: _____

Next contact date: _____

Customer Call Follow-Up Sheet

Prospect's Name: _____

Date: _____

Products/Services Required: _____

_____

_____

Description of Conversation: _____

_____

_____

Date of follow-up call: _____

Next contact date: _____

Prospect's Name: _____

Date: _____

Products/Services Required: _____

_____

_____

Description of Conversation: _____

_____

_____

Date of follow-up call: _____

Next contact date: _____

Prospect's Name: _____

Date: _____

Products/Services Required: _____

_____

_____

Description of Conversation: _____

_____

_____

Date of follow-up call: _____

Next contact date: _____

Prospect's Name: _____

Date: _____

Products/Services Required: _____

_____

_____

Description of Conversation: _____

_____

_____

Date of follow-up call: _____

Next contact date: _____

Prospect's Name: _____

Date: _____

Products/Services Required: _____

_____

_____

Description of Conversation: _____

_____

_____

Date of follow-up call: _____

Next contact date: _____

Prospect's Name: _____

Date: _____

Products/Services Required: _____

_____

_____

Description of Conversation: _____

_____

_____

Date of follow-up call: _____

Next contact date: _____

Daily Time Analysis Sheet

Use this time analysis sheet for one week to track how your time is spent, the make changes as you see fit to make the most productive use of your time.

Time	Activity
5:00 A.M.	_____
5:30 A.M.	_____
6:00 A.M.	_____
6:30 A.M.	_____
7:00 A.M.	_____
7:30 A.M.	_____
8:00 A.M.	_____
8:30 A.M.	_____
9:00 A.M.	_____
9:30 A.M.	_____
10:00 A.M.	_____
10:30 A.M.	_____
11:00 A.M.	_____
11:30 A.M.	_____
Noon	_____
12:30 P.M.	_____
1:00 P.M.	_____
1:30 P.M.	_____
2:00 P.M.	_____

Time	Activity
2:30 P.M.	_____
3:00 P.M.	_____
3:30 P.M.	_____
4:00 P.M.	_____
4:30 P.M.	_____
5:00 P.M.	_____
5:30 P.M.	_____
6:00 P.M.	_____
6:30 P.M.	_____
7:00 P.M.	_____
7:30 P.M.	_____
8:00 P.M.	_____
8:30 P.M.	_____
9:00 P.M.	_____
9:30 P.M.	_____
10:00 P.M.	_____
10:30 P.M.	_____
11:00 P.M.	_____

Number of Hours Spent:

Work: _____

Phone: _____

Internet: _____

Meetings: _____

Customer Contact: _____

Meals: _____

Quality Time with

Family Members: _____

Personal Time: _____

Daily Time Analysis Sheet

Use this time analysis sheet for one week to track how your time is spent, then make changes as you see fit to make the most productive use of your time.

Time	Activity
5:00 A.M.	_____
5:30 A.M.	_____
6:00 A.M.	_____
6:30 A.M.	_____
7:00 A.M.	_____
7:30 A.M.	_____
8:00 A.M.	_____
8:30 A.M.	_____
9:00 A.M.	_____
9:30 A.M.	_____
10:00 A.M.	_____
10:30 A.M.	_____
11:00 A.M.	_____
11:30 A.M.	_____
Noon	_____
12:30 P.M.	_____
1:00 P.M.	_____
1:30 P.M.	_____
2:00 P.M.	_____

Time	Activity
2:30 P.M.	_____
3:00 P.M.	_____
3:30 P.M.	_____
4:00 P.M.	_____
4:30 P.M.	_____
5:00 P.M.	_____
5:30 P.M.	_____
6:00 P.M.	_____
6:30 P.M.	_____
7:00 P.M.	_____
7:30 P.M.	_____
8:00 P.M.	_____
8:30 P.M.	_____
9:00 P.M.	_____
9:30 P.M.	_____
10:00 P.M.	_____
10:30 P.M.	_____
11:00 P.M.	_____

Number of Hours Spent:

Work: _____

Phone: _____

Internet: _____

Meetings: _____

Customer Contact: _____

Meals: _____

Quality Time with
Family Members: _____

Personal Time: _____

Daily Time Analysis Sheet

Use this time analysis sheet for one week to track how your time is spent, the make changes as you see fit to make the most productive use of your time.

Time	Activity
5:00 A.M.	_____
5:30 A.M.	_____
6:00 A.M.	_____
6:30 A.M.	_____
7:00 A.M.	_____
7:30 A.M.	_____
8:00 A.M.	_____
8:30 A.M.	_____
9:00 A.M.	_____
9:30 A.M.	_____
10:00 A.M.	_____
10:30 A.M.	_____
11:00 A.M.	_____
11:30 A.M.	_____
Noon	_____
12:30 P.M.	_____
1:00 P.M.	_____
1:30 P.M.	_____
2:00 P.M.	_____

Time	Activity
2:30 P.M.	_____
3:00 P.M.	_____
3:30 P.M.	_____
4:00 P.M.	_____
4:30 P.M.	_____
5:00 P.M.	_____
5:30 P.M.	_____
6:00 P.M.	_____
6:30 P.M.	_____
7:00 P.M.	_____
7:30 P.M.	_____
8:00 P.M.	_____
8:30 P.M.	_____
9:00 P.M.	_____
9:30 P.M.	_____
10:00 P.M.	_____
10:30 P.M.	_____
11:00 P.M.	_____

Number of Hours Spent:

Work: _____

Phone: _____

Internet: _____

Meetings: _____

Customer Contact: _____

Meals: _____

Quality Time with
Family Members: _____

Personal Time: _____

Daily Time Analysis Sheet

Use this time analysis sheet for one week to track how your time is spent, the make changes as you see fit to make the most productive use of your time.

Time   Activity

5:00 A.M. _____

5:30 A.M. _____

6:00 A.M. _____

6:30 A.M. _____

7:00 A.M. _____

7:30 A.M. _____

8:00 A.M. _____

8:30 A.M. _____

9:00 A.M. _____

9:30 A.M. _____

10:00 A.M. _____

10:30 A.M. _____

11:00 A.M. _____

11:30 A.M. _____

Noon _____

12:30 P.M. _____

1:00 P.M. _____

1:30 P.M. _____

2:00 P.M. _____

Time	Activity
2:30 P.M.	_____
3:00 P.M.	_____
3:30 P.M.	_____
4:00 P.M.	_____
4:30 P.M.	_____
5:00 P.M.	_____
5:30 P.M.	_____
6:00 P.M.	_____
6:30 P.M.	_____
7:00 P.M.	_____
7:30 P.M.	_____
8:00 P.M.	_____
8:30 P.M.	_____
9:00 P.M.	_____
9:30 P.M.	_____
10:00 P.M.	_____
10:30 P.M.	_____
11:00 P.M.	_____

Number of Hours Spent:

Work: _____

Phone: _____

Internet: _____

Meetings: _____

Customer Contact: _____

Meals: _____

Quality Time with

Family Members: _____

Personal Time: _____

Daily Time Analysis Sheet

Use this time analysis sheet for one week to track how your time is spent, then make changes as you see fit to make the most productive use of your time.

Time	Activity
5:00 A.M.	_____
5:30 A.M.	_____
6:00 A.M.	_____
6:30 A.M.	_____
7:00 A.M.	_____
7:30 A.M.	_____
8:00 A.M.	_____
8:30 A.M.	_____
9:00 A.M.	_____
9:30 A.M.	_____
10:00 A.M.	_____
10:30 A.M.	_____
11:00 A.M.	_____
11:30 A.M.	_____
Noon	_____
12:30 P.M.	_____
1:00 P.M.	_____
1:30 P.M.	_____
2:00 P.M.	_____

Time	Activity
2:30 P.M.	_____
3:00 P.M.	_____
3:30 P.M.	_____
4:00 P.M.	_____
4:30 P.M.	_____
5:00 P.M.	_____
5:30 P.M.	_____
6:00 P.M.	_____
6:30 P.M.	_____
7:00 P.M.	_____
7:30 P.M.	_____
8:00 P.M.	_____
8:30 P.M.	_____
9:00 P.M.	_____
9:30 P.M.	_____
10:00 P.M.	_____
10:30 P.M.	_____
11:00 P.M.	_____

Number of Hours Spent:

Work: _____

Phone: _____

Internet: _____

Meetings: _____

Customer Contact: _____

Meals: _____

Quality Time with
Family Members: _____

Personal Time: _____

Goal Sheet

Yearly Goals

Work: _____

Home: _____

Personal: _____

Financial: _____

Community: _____

Spiritual: _____

Monthly Goals

Work: _____

Home: _____

Personal: _____

Financial: _____

Community: _____

Spiritual: _____

Weekly Goals

Work: _____

Home: _____

Personal: _____

Financial: _____

Community: _____

Spiritual: _____

Daily Goals

Work: _____

Home: _____

Personal: _____

Financial: _____

Community: _____

Spiritual: _____

Prioritized Yearly Goals for Work and Home Life

Work

Priority 1: _____

_____

Priority 2: _____

_____

Priority 3: _____

_____

Home

Priority 1: _____

_____

Priority 2: _____

_____

Priority 3: _____

_____

Sales Rejection Analysis Sheet

Prospect's Name: _____

Date: _____

Products/Services Rejected: _____

_____

At What Step in the Process: _____

_____

Reason: _____

_____

What I could have done: _____

_____

Prospect's Name: _____

Date: _____

Products/Services Rejected: _____

_____

At What Step in the Process: _____

_____

Reason: _____

_____

What I could have done: _____

_____

Prospect's Name: _____

Date: _____

Products/Services Rejected: _____

_____

At What Step in the Process: _____

_____

Reason: _____

_____

What I could have done: _____

_____

Prospect's Name: _____

Date: _____

Products/Services Rejected: _____

_____

At What Step in the Process: _____

_____

Reason: _____

_____

What I could have done: _____

_____

Prospect's Name: _____

Date: _____

Products/Services Rejected: _____

_____

At What Step in the Process: _____

_____

Reason: _____

_____

What I could have done: _____

_____

Prospect's Name: _____

Date: _____

Products/Services Rejected: _____

_____

At What Step in the Process: _____

_____

Reason: _____

_____

What I could have done: _____

_____

Index

Trends, 121, 128–29, 153–55, 160–61
Truth, 232–33
Twain, Mark, 56

U

Unethical practices, 97, 229–31
Uniqueness, xiv, 11, 148–51

V

Value, adding, 126–29, 251
Values, 179, 227–33
Verbal communication, 10–11. *See also* Communication skills
Video presentations, 150
Viral marketing, 209, 242
Vision statements, 30–33. *See also* Goals
Visual aids, 139–41
Visualization, 21–22, 223–24, 249–50

W

Wall Street Journal, 154, 156
Web sites, 10, 142–43, 207–9, 237–45. *See also* Internet
Weblogs, 4, 143–44, 237–38
Win-win situations, 179–80
Word-of-mouth advertising, 80–81, 163–67, 205–6, 209
Word-of-net promotions, 242
Workstation organization, 48–49, 199–201

Y

"Yes" factor, 92–93, 163–64

The Everything® Career Guide Series

Helpful handbooks written by experts.

THE
EVERYTHING®
GUIDE TO BEING A
PARALEGAL

Secrets to a successful career!

Steven W. Schneider
Attorney-at-Law

Trade Paperback
ISBN: 1-59337-583-2
$14.95 ($19.95 CAN)

THE
EVERYTHING®
GUIDE TO BEING A
REAL ESTATE AGENT

FOR SALE
SOLD

Secrets to a successful career!

Shahri Masters
Author of The Everything® Homeselling Book, 2nd Edition

Trade Paperback
ISBN: 1-59337-432-1
$14.95 ($19.95 CAN)

THE
EVERYTHING®
GUIDE TO STARTING
AND RUNNING A
RESTAURANT

RESTAURANT

Secrets to a successful business!

Ronald Lee, Restaurateur

Trade Paperback
ISBN: 1-59337-433-X
$14.95 ($19.95 CAN)

THE
EVERYTHING®
GUIDE TO CAREERS IN
HEALTH CARE

Find the job that's right for you

Kathy Quan, R.N., B.S.N., P.H.N.

Trade Paperback
ISBN: 1-59337-725-8
$14.95 ($19.95 CAN)